To Don and Our Children

# FOSTER PARENTING

# YOUNG CHILDREN

## Guidelines from a Foster Parent

### Evelyn H. Felker

SCHOOL OF
CALIFORNIA PROFESSIONAL
PSYCHOLOGY
LOS ANGELES

F-51

Child Welfare League of America
67 Irving Place New York, N.Y. 10003

*3rd Printing 1975*

© Copyright 1974 by the Child Welfare League of America, Inc. All rights reserved. No part of this book may be reproduced in any form by any electronic or mechanical means, including information storage and retrieval systems, without the written permission of the publisher, except by a reviewer, who may quote brief passages in a review.

Library of Congress Catalog Card Number: 73-93885
ISBN 0-87868-119-1

# PUBLISHER'S PREFACE

Despite the Child Welfare League's hopes and searching, a literature for foster parents, written by foster parents, was for many years exceedingly scarce. The coming of the foster parent association movement, with its stimulus to foster parent education, provided both an exchange of information and a sense of competence, as well as practice in communication. It also gave rise to new hope on our part that the development of useful foster parent publications would not be far behind. As if to prove the point, Evelyn Felker's manuscript arrived.

Here is a work that bespeaks long experience, well thought out, well practiced, and simply told. It takes in all aspects of the foster parent's particular role with young children, through application, daily care, the biological parents, the caseworker and the agency, and the foster parent association. Above all, it speaks to life as a foster family—foster parents and their own children—a life style whose special values transcend those of any other kind of family. Foster families know when it is one of their own with whom they talk. In that knowledge the League makes this work available, with great pride and pleasure.

Carl Schoenberg
Director of Publications, CWLA

# Contents

# INTRODUCTION

An early record of a foster care arrangement occurs in the Biblical account of the life of Moses, the Liberator of the Israelites. It is brief and to the point: "Take this child away, and nurse it for me, and I will give thee thy wages."* How ambiguous was the situation of that foster mother. Moses was her child, yet she was to be paid to care for him and the time would come when she must surrender him to another family. Judging from the man Moses became, she did her job well.

Foster parents and child form their new relationship in a situation that still is highly confusing. I think it helps to spell out some of these ambiguous elements. They will not go away, but you will be aware of them and better able to live with them.

In most cases you will be paid to care for the child. This is a contradiction of the parent-child relationship in our society, where the child is to be provided for out of a sense of love and responsibility. Although at times it would seem much simpler to keep money out of the foster care situation, I do not think it would be better.

When we were considering our first foster child arrangement, money was a genuine problem. We felt that we had time, energy and room for another child; we had only one child and did not expect others. We did not want to rear our daughter as an only child, and would have preferred adoption. Financially, adoption was out of the question and we were counseled to look into foster care arrangements.

---

* The story is given in the second chapter of Exodus. The quotation is from the King James Version of the Bible.

There are many families who would welcome another child but need financial help to manage it. I am glad foster care makes this possible. That you will be given money to meet the costs of caring for him will not erase the need to care for the child out of a sense of love and responsibility.

The temporary nature of the arrangement adds another confusing factor to foster care. A parent-child relationship is supposed to be forever. Even when parent and child become two adults, our society defines a special relationship between them. Foster care is temporary, and you and the child know it. Even if the arrangement lasts for years, legal and social distinctions are maintained, and they make your task, if not more difficult, at least different.

There is an encouragement here. Foster care is temporary and I think a parent can learn to regard this as an asset and make it an asset to the child. Most parents are inclined to see their children somewhat as an extension of themselves. Even a parent who does not wish to tie his children up for life finds himself hoping they will fulfill some of his unfinished dreams. I believe it is easier to let the foster child be himself and dream his own dreams.

Sometimes we get so involved in our children's lives that we overreact to their successes and failures, to their joys and disappointments. Too great a part of our lives is invested in them and when they leave (as of course they must) our lives may seem pointless. I think you can enjoy a foster child and share his life without so great a danger of getting too wrapped up in him; the time factor makes you realize that you must make the most of this day with him and enjoy it—soon he will be gone out of your life.

The temporary nature of foster care also affects the matter of rewards. Parents sometimes accept more misery in a situation than is good for either parent or child in the expectation that things are going to get better and it will all be worth it in the golden tomorrow. We try to avoid this attitude with foster care. Life must be lived within acceptable limits now. When the child leaves, the books are balanced and you must be able to feel that what you did was worth doing regardless of how the future turns out for the child. The child needed a home, family, love—you provided these for the time you could, and it was good.

A third ambiguity arises from the fact that two other persons are also this child's parents. Regardless of how much or how little they are involved in the present life of the child, they do exist for him and for you. The preschool child may seem quite willing to forget them. You may not do so. According to the circumstances of each individual case, you must be prepared to acknowledge and cooperate with these parents. This, too, can be an asset to the child. Rather than two parents, he now has four adults who may be willing to love him and share the responsibility for his well-being. If his parents are unable or unwilling to be his parents in any helpful way, he has you to meet some of his needs and to help him come to an understanding and acceptance of his parents as he matures.

In the midst of these ambiguities and contradictions, this is the way we have come to regard foster children. No child "belongs" to his parents. Children born to you, children adopted by you, children you care for in your home are not property. Children live in a parent-child relationship to you regardless of how they happened to arrive in your home. In the case of foster children, their natural parents do not own them either. And at least temporarily the natural parent-child relationship has been broken physically, since the child does not live at home. This fact leaves these parents with many complications to work through. Later we consider ways you can help them, but your primary responsibility is to act and react as the parent in the parent-child relationship. The ramifications of this commitment will be many; it will both simplify and complicate your life. This commitment is the basis upon which this book is written. You are the mother or the father in the house. You may be "aunt" or "grandpa" for some reason in the mind and mouth of the child, but he will accept your role as parent if you accept it.

What is a parent anyhow?

He is the guardian of the physical, intellectual, social and spiritual well-being of the child. The concept of guardian in our society carries the idea of a treasure to be protected and preserved. In the simple baptismal rite of the church where our children were baptized, the minister asks you: "Do you promise to regard this child as a gift of your Heavenly Father entrusted to your care?" In the current worry over population growth and urban crush, it is sometimes hard to remember that a child—any child—is a beautiful gift placed in our care. A parent so regards a child. He knows the child intimately—he helps him come to know and value himself. He protects the child from harm and is on guard that no thing or person be permitted to hurt this treasure. Having done this job well, the parent willingly gives the child up when the time for guarding is past, or his position is properly taken by another careful guardian.

A parent is also one who brings forth. The word itself is from the Latin *parere*, to bring forth. It referred originally, of course, to the acts of begetting and giving birth to a child. The concept has been enlarged to include the idea of being the source or cause of something. In the biological sense you are not the parent of your foster child. But for this child you can and should be a source—of love, of strength, of physical nurture. It is your privilege to parent in him attitudes and understanding toward himself and other people that will change his life for the better.

A parent is certainly one who loves. In our language the word "love" has come to stand for a wide range of feelings and actions. In his book *Insight and Responsibility*, Erik Erikson uses the term "caring" to discuss the relation between a man and whatever he generates or helps to produce and someday leaves behind. In particular, "Care is the widening concern for what has been generated by love, necessity, or accident; it overcomes the ambivalence adhering to irreversible obligation." This kind of caring finds itself involved in securing for all children what they need, and finds doing this a joy. Erikson does not limit this to parenthood as such, but to all the actions a man takes because he needs to be needed, and because he is needed. At a particular time a particular foster child needs caring from you.

When you agree to be parent to a foster child, you enter a relationship that requires every bit of stamina, intelligence and love available. Take all the help you can get and enjoy each day as it comes.

*THE FOSTER CHILD*

# 1

# Assessing Yourself for Foster Care

Foster care is a fairly vague concept in the mind of the general public. When the idea of taking a foster child was presented to my husband and me, we had little idea of what was involved, whether we could do it, whether we would like doing it. This chapter is intended to help you understand what foster care is, and whether and where you would fit in a foster care program.

(If you are involved now in foster care, read it anyway! You may decide to change the way you go at the job, the kind of care you provide, or the age level with which you work. You may discover that you have resources you are not using, or some you could offer to other foster parents.)

First of all, you should answer the question, "What is involved in foster care?" Reading this book and other material on foster care will help you answer this question, but the range of requirements is so broad that you need specific information as well from the agency that places children in your area. A call to the Department of Public Welfare should put you in touch with someone responsible for foster care of children. Make an appointment to visit the agency and talk at length with a staff member in charge of locating foster homes. Be sure she knows that you are new at this, and feel free to ask all the questions you can think of. Make notes on her answers. The decision to take foster children should not be made on inadequate information.

She may have some questions for you too. I think you should decide before you go whether you wish to be interviewed as a prospective foster parent or as an interested person who may possibly become a prospective foster parent. You can tell her when you make the appointment that you want an idea of what is involved before you and your family consider yourselves prospects.

If you do know enough about foster care in a general way to be fairly certain you want to get involved, you may want to go ahead and talk about your situation too. Be honest and open with her. She is trained to seek out persons who will provide good foster homes, and she needs plenty of accurate information.

Some agencies or foster parent associations have written material spelling out the foster care agreement and the division of responsibilities between you and the agency. Ask for such material, study it when you get home, and if you decide to continue, ask for clarification of anything you don't understand.*

A good source of information about your local foster care program is the foster parent association. The agency can put you in touch with the local group. The foster parents will be glad to have you as a guest at a meeting, answer your questions, and give you a picture of foster care conditions in your community. If you are at all a likely looking candidate, they will probably try to recruit you. If there is no formal association of foster parents, ask the agency if it is permitted to give you the names of persons you could talk to who are currently involved in foster care.

Now that you have sought out information on "What is involved in foster care?" you are ready to begin answering the question, "Would we be able to do it?" The agency, too, will need the answer to this question, so if you make this inventory of your resources yourself, you will be ready for the caseworker when she calls.

**Do you have room for another child?** The caseworker who first investigated our home remarked that she was looking for "emotional room for a child" more than for physical space. I now understand better what she meant than I did at the time. It is of course necessary to have a place to sleep and a place to play. For an older child, it is also a matter of a reasonable degree of privacy. But room should involve more. The older child should not be made to feel like an intruder. In the case of the preschool child, emotional room may mean something different. Matt came to live with us just after his fourth birthday. He was a beautiful boy, full of life and mischief. Ruth, our daughter, "adopted" him, and the plan was that he would sleep in her room. But every night for 6 months he had to be put to bed on the living-room couch. He simply could not close his eyes and go to sleep if she were in

---

* The Appendix contains a sample listing of such responsibilities, taken from an association handbook.

the room. If she left the room to give him a chance to settle for the night, he proceeded to tear the room to pieces. So someone sat in the darkened livingroom with him until he went to sleep, and when Ruth was ready for bed she moved him in with her. Temporarily, "room for Matt" meant the family living-room, which happened to be little used during the evening, and a share of Ruth's room. Of course, if he were becoming a permanent member of the family a different solution would have been necessary—maybe a room of his own.

I think emotional room for a child means a willingness on the part of the whole family to adapt to the needs of a child, whatever they may be, without a lot of grumbling and grudging. You walk around those extra toys; ignore the clothes chest in the corner that doesn't really fit the color scheme. (Eventually you will get around to painting it, maybe.) It means willingness to alter family space, schedules and planning to fit another child.

**Can you accept a mess?** In considering the physical aspects of room, you should also consider whether you can put up with having your new rugs puddled on, and the furniture hacked up a bit. Children are hard on furniture, and some foster kids are extra hard. Can you tolerate a fair degree of mess and noise and destructiveness? Your own children learned your rules over a period of time. You can't drop all these rules on a foster child at once, and much damage can be done before he has adjusted to reasonable regulations.

For example, in our home we use the back door routinely for trips in and out of the yard. This saves wear and tear on the carpet and cleaning for mother. If you are extra dirty, you clean up in the basement shower. We cut the laundry load by hanging towels up and using them over. We seldom eat in the living room. Nothing earthshaking—just family rules to make things last a little longer and save work. It would certainly be unreasonable to expect a new foster child to absorb the rules the first day. He will be busy trying to adapt to more important aspects of living with you. So can you take a catsup stain on the carpet and grass stains on your good towels?

The physical aspects can be summarized from the agency's standpoint. Local rules vary and state or city health departments sometimes have regulations designed to assure minimum standards for living conditions. In general, the caseworker will be looking for a normally clean, safe and well-managed household.

**Consider the physical health of your family.** The agency will no doubt require both parents to have a physical examination. Some procedures such as chest X rays and blood tests also may be required. You should take stock of your physical condition and that of the children in the family. Care of children is hard work, and your health and special needs of other members of the household will affect the decision as to the age of the child you take.. There are many children in foster care who have need of special health care. One of these might fit ideally into your home.

**How stable is your family?** After considering the physical resources your family can offer, consider its stability as a family. No real-life family is without problems, and the agency will expect normal ups and downs and turmoil in your home. But the care of foster children places extra strains upon a home situation. Try to appraise the situation in advance. Is the level of communication in your family good enough so that problems are openly discussed and acted upon? There will be a new batch of problems to discuss with the arrival of your new child. Are your present children getting along together reasonably well? It will be easy afterward to forget problems that already existed and blame the new child for any and all troubles (maybe not out loud, but mentally). Is any of your children experiencing difficulties in school the source of which you are unable to determine? Are you having delinquency or truancy problems? Another child in the home may make helping your child more difficult and the foster child may get involved in the problem. It is important to discuss such considerations with the caseworker. Placement of a child may still be possible by taking care to find the right child.

In connection with family stability, I want to stress the importance of the quality of the husband-wife relationship. Little positive help can be offered to the foster child unless both parents agree that fostering is a worthwhile use of the family resources. You will want to counsel and support each other; you will need each other's insight into difficult situations. The bulk of the extra physical care of a child will rest with the foster mother, and there is a tendency in foster care procedures to deal almost exclusively with the foster mother. In the article "Foster Fatherhood: the Untapped Resource," Leo Davids* deals with some of the assets a foster father can offer. Do both of you want to get involved in foster care and are you prepared to work together in making a success of this experience? Are you generally getting along well together? Older foster children can exploit a weak relationship between the foster parents—with great harm to foster parents and foster child.

Some foster children persistently seek exclusive attention. They seem to feel they must test the strength of your love for them by requiring that you do not show love to someone else. Whatever the reason for this, it can cause problems in the family relationships. Sometimes one foster parent becomes isolated from the interactions going

---

* *Child Welfare*, February 1973.

on between the other parent and child, or occasionally a child in the family resents the exclusive nature of the attention being given a foster child. It helps to recognize the problem and know that it arises fairly frequently.

**How are you doing now as parents?** Do you feel that you can evaluate yourself and your relationship to your children and conclude that you are doing a good job as parents? You will almost certainly experience some severe testing of your confidence in your abilities as you become foster parents. It helps to have the feeling that you are doing or have done a pretty successful job of being parents. Of course this child is different and many other factors enter the situation, but have you satisfied yourself that you can rear a child?

**How do your children feel about your plan?** Having agreed as husband and wife that you would like to try foster care, you should involve your children in the process of exploring the plan and how family members could fit in. This is not a matter of a children's veto. Your children should be willing to give a fair hearing to a plan their parents have agreed upon. If you were correct in your evaluation of the stability and quality of your family life, their lively interest in the project is almost certain.

Try to give the children a clear picture of what kinds of changes foster care will bring to the family. Be sure they know that money is involved. Our children tended to find this puzzling, and we explained to them the rationale behind foster care payments. (Have you fully accepted this aspect yourself?) Use plenty of examples of the kinds of situations in which the foster child's presence will affect their lives. You will not be free to help as much at school perhaps, or sometimes an older daughter will have to babysit. Try to get across to your children the reasons why you feel foster care would be worthwhile for your family. Tell them about the foster child's needs and what you believe your family has to offer. Let them talk too! This is not a one-time, "big deal" conference and it's settled. Encourage questions or bring up the subject several times over a period of days. Our children went with us to visit the agency after the decision was made. That might be practical and worthwhile for your family too. Children and adults are likely to cooperate in plans they had a genuine share in making.

Another part of planning for foster care involves choosing the right child for your family. You will have to explore carefully the kind of child for whom you are best able to provide a home. This exploration should be done with the person who enlists you as foster parents, but there are some aspects you can consider in advance of her discussion with you.

**For what age child are you looking?** Assuming you have children of your own at home, what are their ages? There are some periods in a child's development when there are considerable turmoil and uncertainty in your relationship with him and in his relationship with siblings and others. Early adolescence tends to be one of these periods. I think that as a rule adding another child in the same age range is not a good idea at this age period. Your difficulties and those of the children may be multiplied by four instead of two. Early adolescence is also an age when a child is beginning to see himself as moving toward adult roles. He may be very ready to commit himself to the care and love of a preschool child.

How busy is the life of your older children? Do they really have time to help you much more than they do at present? Are you going to expect a lot of babysitting if you take a very young child, and will this cut into study hours or dating and be resented after a few weeks? Think about the age of your own children as you try to determine what age foster child you would like to parent.

**What are your local schools like?** Many foster children have been through experiences that have caused them to fall behind academically. Some have not had early-life experiences that prepare them as well as children in your neighborhood are prepared. What can your school offer in the way of remedial tutoring or special help to foster children? Is there academic snobbery about the schools in your area that the children in general have picked up? This can be hard on a transfer student, especially on a foster child.

**What special community services are available to you?** Several years ago friends of ours undertook the foster care of a child who was thought to be mentally retarded. Physically he was beautiful, and a bundle of misdirected energy. Purdue University makes clinic services available to foster children, and the family was in a position to take advantage of these. The child has now reached the normal range of development for his age. Accurate diagnosis, professional help, and loving family care have combined to recover a child. Other children need physical therapy or extensive speech work. Do you live where getting these for the child would be practical?

**Crossing race lines.** Depending upon the area in which you live, there may be need for homes for children of minority races. Be realistic and fair, not just about your own attitudes but about the attitudes of the school and neighborhood. You may be ready to meet prejudice head on, but is the foster child?

**Special factors in your family?** No two families are exactly alike and you will have to consider fairly subtle problems. One of our first foster children eventually was in need of a permanent home and came back to us for adoption. By the time he was legally our son the idea of being a foster child was painful and unsettling to him. We decided that we would not have children entering and leaving our home. When he was past middle adolescence this no longer was a factor that required much consideration. Before you get into foster care, consider what it may mean to each member of your family, even if some members do not bring up the problem.

**Are you looking for long- or short-term care?** Many children need homes to grow up in. There are early adolescents who need homes until they finish high school. There are children for whom some type of family emergency makes short-term care necessary—perhaps only days or weeks. There are children handicapped in some way who cannot be kept in their own families, but who do not need and would not benefit from institutional care. There are children who need a home to live in while they are evaluated and an adoptive home is being readied. There are children who are taken from their homes while efforts are made to improve the parenting so that the children can return. There are combinations of all these different situations. Which ones look like possibilities for your family?

To illustrate how this section of your inventory works out, our present agreement is to accept one or two children, generally preschool age, on an emergency-call basis, for periods up to 90 days. None of these conditions is an absolute: older children have come; children have stayed longer; sometimes we have time to plan ahead. We have accepted as many as four for a brief stay. The present arrangement suits our family just fine and fills a need of the child care agency. I know of a grandmother in her 70s who takes newborn babies for a few weeks of loving care while homes are readied for their adoption. There are all kinds of possibilities.

**What depth of commitment will you bring to the foster care program?** No thoughtful person assumes that taking on the responsibility of being parent to any child will be easy. Some days it will be extremely hard. There will be times that are good and times when you feel you are making a mess of the whole experience. One conviction keeps me going. I believe that every child is meant to reflect in the world the image of a perfect Creator and that I can have a part in the restoration of that image. We have received children still bearing bruises from parental cruelty. Another child was content to sit blankly and quietly far too long. Others are beautiful and intelligent, but with emotions so out of control that their lives seem one long scream from morning until night.

In a way, it is exciting to work with these children. Often change comes surprisingly fast. A child's personality is remarkably resilient. At other times a much more plodding kind of concern is required. At times little progress is made (perhaps none is expected) and day after day it is one more set of clothes to care for, one more mouth to feed, one more child to get ready for bed. The value of children is such that they are worth your best efforts day after day—and that is what they require.

Now, are you ready to talk to the caseworker as a prospective foster family?

# 2

# Welcoming the Foster Child

Procedures and regulations regarding the placement of a foster child vary with state and even county and according to your understanding with the child care agency. The child may come to you after adequate time for you to prepare for him. He may be clean, neatly dressed and arrive in the company of his mother and a caseworker, perhaps even prepared by a previous visit or two. So our first two children arrived.

If you have agreed to accept children on an emergency basis, children may arrive on notice of a couple hours or less. They may be dirty, dressed in ill-fitting clothes, half-sick, very tired and bewildered by the hardest day of their lives. I suppose most foster child placements fit somewhere between these extremes.

In any case, prepared or not, you and a total stranger have been placed in one of the most intimate relations of our society. Don't be surprised if the shock depresses you. You will probably catch yourself thinking, "Why did I let myself in for this?" But some time before, you took stock of yourself and your situation and made a rational commitment to be parent to a foster child. This is that child, so pitch in and put those resources to work.

**Getting started.** There will not be time for an extended conference over the child's head on the day he arrives at your home. You do need a couple of basic bits of information. Be sure you have written down the name of the caseworker and her phone number. If she is willing, ask her to give you an after-office-hours number, too. Get the name of the child's doctor. Even if you plan to take him to some other doctor, it might be necessary to get prior health information in a hurry. Be sure

15

you have the first name of the child and the nickname he goes by. Agencies may supply a brief written history of the child when he comes, but in some cases there may not have been time to gather this information before placement. It can be mailed to you later. If the caseworker has more than a few sentences of information to give you, ask her to wait while you place the child in the care of another person in another room, or better yet, call her at nap time or later that evening. Half-whispered conferences over the head of the child are frightening for him, and most caseworkers will avoid them. This does not mean the caseworker is unwilling to give you the information.

You will spend the next few days getting acquainted with a new child. Take stock of his physical condition. I like to take a new foster child to see our family doctor within a week or so if the plan calls for him to spend an extended time with us. Of course, if he is sick when he arrives, you will see a doctor right away. But I believe a child should see the doctor who will be treating him before it is an emergency situation. The choice of a doctor for the child is made by the agency and usually the agency is responsible for medical bills. If it makes no particular difference to the agency, it helps to use the same doctor who takes care of your other children. He knows you and you know him, and that takes one set of unknowns out of the situation when illness occurs. Until the situation arises, you may not realize how much more serious illness in a foster child can seem to you. It is a matter partly of not knowing him. Let me give an example. When our daughter Linda was a toddler, she ran a temperature for the slightest reason. I knew that early in a cold she could appear very sick and have a temperature of 103 degrees. With ordinary care, 48 hours later there would be only the tail end of a head cold. But I certainly would not advocate waiting 48 hours to see what happened the first time a foster child ran that kind of fever. You eventually will learn what his symptoms mean, how sick he is, how well he throws off infections. You will have to be extra cautious at first.

In this day of routine immunizations, it is surprising how many children have not had the protective shots they need. If the records you receive do not show he has had them, check on his immunization history and arrange for him to have the ones he needs.

Even preschool children need dental attention. The children currently in our home have cavities and appear to have gum problems. Once again, most agencies will be glad to arrange for the payments, but your initiative is required in making the appointments and getting the child there.

**Eating.** If you have a family to which you are adding another child, meals present no particular problem unless the child won't eat. I try at first to serve simple foods familiar to most children (hot dogs, apple-sauce, peanut butter and jelly sandwiches) and make no fuss about how much or how little he eats, what his table manners are like, etc. There will be time to consider this later. Don't upset his system by introducing foods he may not be used to, or force him to eat what he does not want. Moving into a stranger's house might take away your appetite, too. Chances are that in a few days he will be eating and drinking in a normal pattern (for him).

**Sleep.** Getting a young foster child to bed the first few nights is likely to be the most harrowing part of the whole experience. I don't think there are any ways to avoid this problem completely. You will have to be patient and kind, and try to understand how frightened and lonely he feels. I would not hesitate to leave lights on, let him sleep with an older child, take toys to bed, or do anything else within reason that gets him to bed those first few nights. You may be afraid of starting something you don't want to continue. You can deal with that much better later, when he feels more at home with you. In the meantime it is useless to try to set up good sleep habits with an exhausted child who is too terrified to go to sleep.

**Clothing.** The simplest rule for clothing the foster child is to try to keep him dressed about the way you dress your own children, or the way children in the neighborhood are dressed. Rules about respon-sibility for clothing budgets vary with the agency. The procedure for your agency will be in its handbook, or can be discussed with the caseworker.

Older children need an individualistic approach to clothing, but over the years we have found it worthwhile to collect an assortment of clothing for boys and girls from infant to about age 10 (the age range of children for whom we normally care). Most of the clothes have been given to us by friends who are glad to see them put to use. These are good, sturdy clothes, attractive and comfortable in style. I mend and wash them and put them away sorted by size. Separate chests hold different age groups; different drawers hold pajamas, underwear, sum-mer and winter clothing. An extra closet under the eaves holds play jackets and better coats. Within a few minutes, one of the girls or I can get together an outfit for a new child.

There are two or three reasons we do it this way. Child welfare budgets are limited and it seems sensible to recycle clothing and save the funds to give the children other services of higher priority than new clothing. Also, it is hard to take a strange new child into stores on a shopping trip, and hard to fit him by guess if you leave him with a sitter and go to find him a wardrobe. Shopping in your own cupboards is much easier! It gives you a chance to involve your friends and others in the needs of these children—to make them aware of the foster care program. We need all the public support we can get. Children especially can and do enjoy helping in this way. An appeal to my Junior Girl Scout troop for a particular size or need never fails to bring an enthusiastic response, and it is a concrete way the scouts can practice their promise. Purdue University students have supplied beautiful clothing for the children. (This method of supplying a wardrobe would not be acceptable for older children, especially teenagers.)

If I am given something that involves delicate laundering or that will be ruined easily as the child wears it, I pass it on to someone else. For me it is a matter of the best use of time. For the child, I am considering the fact that I do not want to fuss at him unnecessarily, and that I want him to have clothing that by reasonable care can be kept attractive. I don't want to sound too utilitarian. Little boys and girls like to look nice, and our older children love to dress them up. If we need clothes, we ask for them. If the child is old enough to show any interest or preference, I keep his clothing where he can choose it himself to get dressed in the morning.

A word about diapers. I also keep on hand five dozen diapers and an assortment of plastic panties in various sizes. You might prefer disposable diapers, but I find cloth diapers very adaptable for an infant or a 4-year-old who has relapses when he is upset. The first few days or weeks of a placement is not the time to get into a struggle over toilet training, and it is easier to be relaxed about it if you can put him in diapers and forget it for a while. Don't be afraid of undoing his training. As soon as he is able to stay clean and dry again he will want to do so.

**Toys.** The overriding requirements in toys for young children should be safety and sturdiness. Safety, of course, for all children, and sturdiness especially for foster children. At best or worst you are going to be amazed at the wear and tear some children can put on toys. Absolutely indestructible trucks fall apart in their hands. Stuffed animals get an ear chewed off in minutes while you are answering the phone. Even the tricycle that survived three children gives up the ghost the second week. So be prepared to budget for replacements as necessary, and don't conclude that this child is doing it on purpose! Once again, solicit your friends, scout troop, Sunday school class. Keep only that which meets your requirement of safety and sturdiness. I think fragile toys, in addition to presenting extra hazards, tend to encourage destructiveness in the child. The toy should be able to take some punishment until he finds out it is really more fun to play with it as the designer intended. Especially if you will have a succession of children, you may want to consider how easy toys will be to disinfect or keep reasonably clean. Young children tend to mouth toys a lot when they are in a new situation or feeling disturbed.

**Furniture.** Another thing we have collected over the years has been an assortment of preschool furniture. Most of it is hand-me-down. I have extra chests for storing clothing, a full-size crib and two portable cribs, a high chair and a couple of youth chairs and a playpen with pad. If you have the room, it is worthwhile to keep some equipment like this on hand. It can be had for the asking, or very inexpensively in secondhand stores, and it simplifies enormously the routines of caring for children under 5.

**Family adjustments.** Most foster children are placed in homes where there are already children living at home. The adjustments involved in welcoming a new member to the family are multiplied by the number of family members. After an interruption of several years our family decided to try foster care again as a family, and our children share continuously in our successes and failures. All of us agree that to share our home with foster children has added much that is good to our family life. But the work is still hard, the adjustments are numerous and sometimes difficult. We have at present at home a 4-year-old boy and girls 9, 12 and 16. From a practical point the 4-year-old is the most difficult to handle during each adjustment period. Perhaps you can use some of these ideas if you have preschool children.

We give Jeff some warning to expect a new visitor. We make clear from the start that the new child will not live with us "forever." This is a word Jeff uses and it seems to have reasonably accurate meaning for him. We try to give him some idea of the child's age in relation to his own. His acceptance of the child varies with its age. Several weeks with a newborn were followed by the arrival of a 2-year-old and a 3-year-old. His question when I told him they were coming says a lot. "Can it walk?" He had discovered that babies took a lot of time and attention but were unsatisfactory playmates.

Jeff is a sturdy, medium-active 4-year-old with an even disposition. He falls promptly to sleep for at least an hour's nap, sleeps well 10 hours a night, eats with evident enjoyment, plays well with other children but is inclined to retreat before open aggression. He is what mothers refer to as "an easy child." His sisters are good to him but have a combination of enough selfishness and good sense not to overprotect or pamper him. All in all, he finds life pretty comfortable. When a child near his age enters his world he is at first delighted. But if that child happens to be a biting, clawing, fighter with mayhem on his mind, Jeff is confused. While we are trying to get acquainted with the new child and settle into routines with him, we attempt to be certain that Jeff gets some time away from the child. After a particularly trying morning, he may come to me and ask when the children are going home. I explain again in terms he can at least partly understand why they are here and what we want to do. When things get bad, he may go next door for an hour or two of loving attention from Grandma. Dad may take him to McDonald's for an order of french fries, or he may go to play with a neighbor friend. He has to learn to tolerate competition, to handle some frustration. But we try not to expect too much from him in the very place that should be his special sanctuary. A happy, secure 4-year-old can help a foster child, and Jeff has offered small-boy comfort many times when mine has been refused.

Shirley is 9 now and, as with her older sister, much of her time is spent at school and with friends, so that there is less need for the minute-by-minute adjustments Jeff makes in sharing his toys, treats, and especially his mother. For children 2 and under, Shirley can take responsibility for helping in their care. Older preschool children are the hardest for her, since she is not experienced enough to know how to win their cooperation. They also are more likely to be attracted by her prized possessions and are able to open doors and climb on chairs to reach them. Shirley enjoys a child near her age, and the worries and fears of school children seem much less with her in the house to be a playmate.

Both Linda and Ruth are experienced babysitters and they adjust to a new child by assuming part of the mothering task. We find that the extent of mothering that happens is closely related to the disposition of the child. The girls of course will do what must be done for any child, but some children are more appealing, and this makes a difference. They also can and do assume a greater share of the cooking, housework and shopping than when I am not so busy.

Since all of us tend to enjoy quiet and time for talking and reading, the hardest children for all are the extremely noisy ones. Our present foster children are 2 and 3 years old. They believe it is necessary to scream at the top of their lungs for their wishes and continue the screaming until the demand is met. If we cannot understand what is wanted or do not grant the request, loud, hoarse screaming may continue for an hour, with the other joining in. It is a difficult problem, and hard on family life. It is not possible to hold a conversation while the children are awake; just the noise level is wearing. We are trying to solve the problem and feel some progress is being made, but it may be necessary to discuss with the agency separating the children, since so much of the behavior is imitative, and because two children make more noise than one!

The last example illustrates the need to be reasonable about the adjustments required of your family. They can tolerate a pretty bad situation for a time but if you are not able to help the foster child to change, something else should be tried for the sake of both foster child and family. On the other hand, experience in giving substantial help to foster children is helping our children to learn compassion and patience. They are learning to sacrifice something for another's welfare, not as martyrs, but with the joy that comes from helping to meet need.

**When a child leaves.** A period of adjustment follows the departure of children. The extra time for hobbies, for catching up on major housework chores, for doing piled-up shopping is welcome. There is a letdown, too. We miss the children. When they have been placed in a good situation, departure is easier. When all concerned have had to settle for marginal solutions, it is more depressing.

We sometimes visit a departed child in his new setting, so that Jeff is satisfied as to what happened to the child. If that is not practical, we talk about the new home, using as an example a child Jeff has visited recently. From the beginning we maintain the habit of speaking of "when," not "if," the child leaves. Naturally, if you do not expect such a departure and it happens, it is sad for everyone. But after all, we do not have a guarantee that we will have a child of our own forever. That is sufficient reason for enjoying each day with a child.

Making a stranger part of your family is not particularly easy, and much of the initiative must come from you if your foster child is not to remain an outsider, rather than participant, in your family's life. Sometimes foster parents feel the child is not trying to fit in or does not want to be included. This may be true, and it may take much love and skill to win him. I have the impression that the older the child, the more likelihood of difficulties in "fitting in," difficulties that seem, at least to you, to be willed by the child.

In the matter of allowances, chores, privileges and opportunities, the general rule is that the agency expects foster children to be treated as your own. Of course you must provide for the same individual differences that occur between your own children, and no one can give you a list of rules to follow.

You also may have to expend some time and energy getting the child settled into the new neighborhood. There is sometimes a good deal of curiosity and prying about the background of a new child who appears in your home. You will need tact of course; the child's background is his story, not yours, and you should protect his privacy. This does not, of course, apply to teachers or others with a need and right to know. If his aggressive play or his shyness is going to present difficulties with neighbor children or their mothers, you should be prepared to stay alert to the situation until he is accepted in the neighborhood. In our neighborhood, the mother closest to the scene handles the problems as she sees fit, and this works remarkably well for our foster children too.

If the first days or weeks seem much harder than you expected, don't be discouraged. We sometimes find ourselves saying, "This adjustment period is the hardest yet!" But it doesn't seem logical that foster care is getting more difficult. Rather, I think that in each case the pleasures of later weeks tend to erase from our minds the difficulties of the initial weeks.

# 3

# Coping With Problems

Before our first daughter was born, a nurse friend advised me to buy and spend time absorbing *Baby and Child Care,* by Dr. Benjamin Spock. I took her advice, and over the years have worn out two paperback copies of the book. It is the best handbook for parents I have read. There are also available excellent books dealing with older children. But most books either tend to assume that you are starting fresh with an infant or deal with children who are for some reason exceptional.

The foster parent is frequently faced with unhappy situations that are not of her making, and must try to improve them. This chapter deals with some of the common areas of difficulty. It assumes that you are familiar with normal child care handling; if not, I suggest you consult a standard handbook on child care for a description of "normal" behavior in the area of difficulty.

These are the problems illustrated: eating habits; bowel and bladder training; sleep; destructiveness; the "too-good" child; and low self-esteem. Discipline is also a problem area, but this requires a chapter by itself.

If you and your own child have worked yourselves into a bind over sleeping or eating, at least you know how you got where you are, or you can stop to figure it out. In foster care, you probably will not know what is behind a certain fear or particular habit, though you may be able to make an educated guess. The common ingredient required for solution of all these problems is patience. As you try some of these suggestions, other possibilities for trial will occur to you. I give some examples; by reading other books you can gleam many other ideas. Many solutions I suggest are not original, and often I cannot remember the source of the idea.

**Eating.** It is not surprising that, since eating forms so basic a part of life, the child who has been living under stress should reflect it in feeding problems.

What I did with Sandy, who arrived at our home just past a year in age, illustrates how not to deal with one type of eating problem. She was thin and pale and we visited a pediatrician within days. He told me that she was suffering from "milk anemia" and asked what she was eating. She wasn't. She was deriving all her nourishment from bottles of milk, which she emptied as soon as they were filled. She carried the empty bottle with her all the time. The doctor told me to take her bottle away, offer a cup and feed her solids. I am sure he expected no such drastic action as I then took. I followed his orders to the letter. Sandy would not touch the cup herself; she would not drink milk from it if I offered it to her. So I mixed extra dry milk with her cereals and puddings, gave her cheese and cottage cheese when she would accept them, and did not offer the cup for weeks. Meals became a struggle. She would eat a reasonable quantity of finely mashed food if we fed it to her slowly, a small spoonful at a time. If we turned away as she finished, she was likely to vomit the whole meal into her lap. She snatched for Linda's bottle, so I weaned Linda too—no problem; she was nearly a year and ready to give up the bottle. After several weeks I offered the cup and Sandy batted it across the kitchen. Three times a day the struggle over meals interfered with her whole relationship to us. Fortunately, an adoptive home became available for her and she was taken out of foster care. I hope her new mother had the sense and patience to correct the damage I had done.

This illustrates one fundamental principle. The method of dealing with a nutritional problem must be reasonably acceptable to the child. If I had explained more fully to the pediatrician how Sandy felt about the bottle, I am sure he could have helped. He could have given iron shots perhaps, and advice on how to go slowly in weaning her. I should have gone back to him when eating became such an issue. In a sense Sandy was a feeding problem when she came to our home. But attempts at solution must not make the problem worse.

Rey had a seemingly innocent eating quirk at 20 months. He adored bananas. Every day he had a banana, sometimes two. But a strong and unpleasant odor clung to Rey, and to anyone who held him. Why all this fuss about a smell? Because it tended to make family members avoid holding him when they were dressed in good clothes or on their way out of the house. And we couldn't very well go around explaining to visitors that he always smelled as if he needed a diaper change. How can a child learn to consider himself lovable if for reasons unknown to him his overtures for affection are rejected? After a few weeks, Rey was ready for placement in long-term foster care. It was his new foster mother who discovered, with her physician, that Rey's high consumption of bananas was the cause of the odor. Although he liked them, apparently he could not properly digest them in such quantities. By this time he was able to ask for many good things and do without the bananas.

It is a good idea to mention eating quirks to the doctor. He is in a position to evaluate their significance to the child's physical health. If the quirk is just a nuisance, it's up to you to decide whether it is important enough to risk substituting one quirk for another that may prove to be worse.

Be sure to check the sections on eating in a child care handbook. I don't know why I didn't follow Spock's advice for Sandy. I have for other children and find that eating problems do respond to his sensible suggestions.

**Bowel and bladder training.** A large proportion of young children who arrive in foster care have been involved in struggles with their parents over bowel and bladder training. You may inherit a problem.

I prefer to do nothing at all about bladder or bowel training until I have established a reasonably strong and loving relationship with the child. Put diapers on him and forget it. If he is smearing, do the best you can to keep his diapers securely pinned, for no one is of a mind to be unemotional about smearing for long and perhaps you shouldn't be. Try to keep him clean and dry. Be matter of fact and kind as you change him, and very gentle.

When you think the child is ready for training arrange to get, probably through the caseworker, some information about his previous experience with training. (It isn't that important if asking questions is going to make the parents feel defensive or upset.) If he is unusually far past control age, you can check with the doctor to make certain there is no physical malfunction.

This is the way we approached training with one child. Joe was about 3½ when he was placed with us. He obviously had control over both bowel and bladder. If he chose to exert himself, he toileted himself for some days without an accident. But he defecated and smeared if I did something he didn't like. Some days he seemed to urinate without the slightest notice of what was going on. We put him in diapers for 3 months. During that time we were careful to change him promptly, handled him especially gently in dressing and undressing him, and often took time to smooth on oil or powder "to make him smell good." From time to time I commented on how different and pleasant it felt to be clean and dry, and how much easier it would be to stay that way when he began using the toilet.

During this period he received a gift of new clothing from his grandmother. Included were several pair of training pants. I guessed from that that Grandma hoped Joe was being trained. When I happened to see her, I thanked her and asked about his previous training experience. She told me that his parents had frequently punished him severely for accidents. Yet neither parent "would bother when he said he wanted to go to the bathroom." This gave us a clue both to his smearing and to the unimportance he seemed to attach to learning to use toilet facilities. I added to my comments to Joe that I would be very pleased, and glad to help him, when he was ready to try using his new big-boy pants instead of diapers.

In his fourth month with us Joe indicated he wanted to try. There were few accidents afterward. I didn't really train him—he decided for himself, as soon as he was able, that he wanted to take this step. We tried to provide a pleasant general atmosphere and encouragement that this was possible and desirable for him to do.

By all means be willing to go slowly. It really isn't much more work in the long run and, as a friend with a late-dry boy once remarked: "They aren't going to ask him when he enters college when he was potty-trained."

**Sleep.** One problem crops out almost universally with the foster children we have known—in one way or another they have difficulty with sleep. For some it simply may be fear of going to sleep in a strange place, and reassurance, plus time to get acquainted, solves the problem. Sleep problems are so common in children that suggestions and solutions abound in child care books. Your problem will probably yield to one of these possibilities. A couple of examples may get you thinking about a solution.

We had one boy who was not afraid of going to sleep *per se*. Tommy could relax and fall asleep easily in your arms. He would crawl around on the floor playing and I would find him in a corner, fast asleep. But awake or asleep he would not be put in a crib. He didn't just cry and fall asleep—he cried in terror, and could maintain that crying far beyond the traditional 15 minutes. The longer he cried, the more upset and less likely to sleep he became. So for several weeks Tommy took his naps on the floor or the sofa or in any convenient set of arms. We moved his crib in with Jeff and sometimes put both of them in at nonsleeping times to play and read for a while. We rocked him soundly to sleep and put him down in a dark room so that he could not see the crib. What particular thing helped we don't know, but

eventually he was napping and sleeping in his crib with no more protest than any other child makes from time to time.

A harder problem is still with us. Perhaps by the time this book is
finished we will have found a way to deal with the night wanderer.
This habit seems fairly common with children about 3 or 4 years old.
The amount of sleep they lose is unimportant. The hazards to themselves, to the house, and to the cookie jar are considerable. At present
the only thing I can suggest is finding some way to assure that someone
hears the child leave his bed, or is on guard when he is awake. Some
sort of escape-proof sleep space is also a suggestion, but we have never
used locked rooms for children. It might be possible to use a crib cov-
ered with net if the child is small enough, but this means the child
cannot make independent trips he may need to make, such as to the
bathroom. If you have a solution you find effective, well, share it!

**Destructiveness** seems to be a problem with many foster children. If
you think the child you are caring for is unusually destructive, look for
the reason before doing much talking about it. We once had a child
who expressed his fears in this way. One time I put him to bed at a
relative's house, without apparent distress on his part. When I went
back in an hour or so to check on him, he was silently sobbing to
himself and had torn his sheet blanket into shreds. Destructiveness?
Rather, a way of telling us how frightened he was. Does the child
know how to play properly with toys? He may need help in getting
started on imaginative play with toys if he has not had them to grow
up with. Does his apparent urge to take apart and wreck things hide a
lively curiosity about how things work? Real alarm clocks or old radios
to take apart with real tools may help. Remember that he learns respect for your things as he learns to love and respect you and value
your feelings. Be sure you treat his things well and do not permit other
children to mishandle them. More comments on coping with destructiveness are in the section on discipline.

**The passive child.** Another kind of problem is the "too-good" child.
Twice we have cared for such children. The first was a toddler. He
was willing to stay out of things and in one place, to do exactly as he
was told, to surrender his toys to other children without a squawk (often not bothering to reach out for another toy). He may have been a
naturally timid child who needed a lot of encouragement. Instead, it
had been convenient to keep him "good," and his attempts to explore
had been severely punished. He responded rapidly to encouragement.
We used no punishment, and removed him gently from dangerous situations. He needed to add "Yes" to his well-learned "No, no."

The other child was in first grade. At home, or with his own mother,
or with the caseworker he was quiet, diffident, passive. It was his

caseworker who first described him as "too good." We were making an
effort to increase his self-confidence and activity level. It was a shock
to meet his teacher for our first conference. After some hemming and
hawing, the teacher informed us that his school behavior was aggressive toward other children, destructive toward school property, and
disobedient toward the teachers. She wondered if he should be in a
special school. We sought advice at once, since we had no experience
in dealing with this problem. A child whose behavior falls into extremely different patterns depending upon his external situation needs
help. If you cannot give it, find someone else to help him. You will
have to be a party to the counseling.

**Low self-esteem.** All of us carry around in our minds pictures of
ourselves that have been formed over years of accepting our own and
others' evaluations of us. The pictures are made up of our ideas of how
we look physically, how we act, and what people think of us. They
may reflect accurately what we are like, or may be much more attractive pictures than are warranted. For instance, we may see ourselves as
younger and slimmer than we are. We may see ourselves as unselfish,
while others may feel we have a martyr attitude. On the other hand,
we may see ourselves as less attractive than we are to others and be
unnecessarily dissatisfied with ourselves.

Generally speaking, it is desirable that self-pictures be reasonably
accurate and that we like ourselves. Naturally, each of us would like to
change some aspects of himself, but sometimes a person holds such a
poor opinion of himself that he is not only unhappy, but is unable to
undertake the changes that might make him like himself better. A foster child can be in such a position.

The self-concept is built to a great extent on a sense of belonging, a
sense of competence, and a sense of worth. Apparently this image of
self begins to form at about 18 months or 2 years, becomes fairly well
fixed as language is acquired, and tends to be stable in the direction in
which it is fixed. A child who thinks well of himself tends to weather
minor crises and continues to think himself a worthwhile person. A
child with a low opinion of himself tends to find things to confirm that
opinion as he grows older. However, it is certainly possible for foster
parents to help a child in this area, and if they do, it will contribute
greatly to his well-being.

Consider first that the self-concept grows out of a sense of belonging. The infant has no thought about such things as "Who am I?" Ideally, his needs are met—he is fed and clothed and loved as a matter of
course. When he begins to walk and talk, limits are set on what he can
do and how totally his demands are met, but in the happy family he is
still loved and wanted. He is encouraged to identify with his family

and he develops a sense of love for that which is "mine" and gladly surrenders some of his selfish gratifications in exchange for the love and sense of belonging he desires. A boy develops pride in his family, and is glad to be identified as "Daddy's boy." When our middle daughter was 3, I was working during most of her play hours and had not met some of her playmates. We went for a walk together one afternoon soon after I left my job. She marched me from sandbox to sandbox and at each one she announced proudly: "This is my Mom, and she can beat any of you."

Now think what happens to the foster child. Usually his early childhood has been far from ideal. Of course, that is true for many children, and they survive and grow into happy, competent adults. But after a number of years of less-than-ideal care, a foster child is taken out of the home where he has developed whatever sense of pride and belonging he could manage, and is placed in a home where he does not feel he belongs. One aspect of his self-concept is under attack.

Think next about the sense of competence. Out of a sense of security that comes from knowing where he belongs, the young child ventures out to explore the world. Every mother of more than one child knows that there is wide variation between children in the family on this measure of willingness to take a chance on something new. But we expect that happy children will try, that their failures will be taken in stride by the family and themselves, and that they will try and try again. Even more important, their successes will be met with praise and encouragement. The gentle prodding of "You can do it" is followed by his shout of triumph, "I did it!" Many foster children have had parents so full of trouble that they have been unable to provide this encouraging atmosphere for their children. If the child is older and has been to school, the mental set he brought there may have helped to make that experience a failure (at least from his point of view) as well. I have seen early elementary school foster children who have already developed a low opinion of their competence to do anything. In some cases this is not a completely innaccurate assessment. They are less competent in many skills than children who have had better early childhood experiences. So the foster child's self-concept is under attack on the dimension of his sense of competence.

The third aspect I mentioned as a building block for self-concept is a sense of worth. The loving care a child receives and the consistent correction of his misdeeds help him develop the feeling that he is a worthwhile person, since important people take such good care of him. That he can do things that other people tell him are "good" things also builds into his thinking the idea that he is worthwhile. Obviously, any number of things can go wrong. He may not receive loving care.

There may not be an effort to help him learn self-control, and he may feel no one cares enough to help him do what is right. He may not learn to do, or there may be no one to praise him for his efforts. He may get the impression that he is worth noticing only when he is making trouble. He may be valued only for what he can do, and receive the impression that when he fails at something he is of lesser value as a person. He may feel that if he were really "worth anything he would not be placed in foster care where someone has to be paid to take care of him." Once again, the self-concept must weather trouble, this time in the area of intrinsic worth.

To describe the problem is to suggest some things you can do as a foster parent to help the child who has low self-esteem. The foster child must begin to develop a sense of belonging. You must help him with this both by what you say and by the kind of care you give him. If he is old enough to want to "belong" to his own family too, you can help him to do that. (Suggestions about this are in the chapter on parental visiting.) In the case of the preschooler, it may be necessary to back up chronologically and give him the kind of care that suits his emotional age.

As you permit him to belong to you, you can also encourage him to learn—to develop competence in specific tasks for which you then praise him. Teach him to give himself credit too, so he won't be too dependent on others' opinions and manipulations. We had a child of almost 4 who refused to have any part in dressing himself. He preferred to lie on the floor and be dressed like an infant. We gently prodded him into doing more and more—first just choosing what he would wear, then standing to be dressed and taking an active part in the process, then helping to put on easier garments. At each stage the end of the dressing process was a trip to the full-length mirror for him to examine and praise the results. Such simple routines can be worked out for other things he needs to learn. Remember to praise each small success, and, if at all possible, to ignore the failures and mistakes. It will be more effective to notice that he got the shirt over his head and one sleeve on, than to comment on the empty sleeve. If the child is older, the school should be involved in an effort to raise his level of competence and self-esteem.

The child's sense of worth will grow partly out of what he senses to be the attitude toward him of those around him. Your feeling that he is a worthwhile child will be communicated to him. This goes back to your basic attitude toward children as being of value, and as worthy of your best efforts in caring for them. Let him know he has a right to this kind of care.

I want to add one caution. The opinion of himself that a child holds should be taken seriously. This is true for various reasons. If he states something such as "I'm no good," and this is consistent with his general attitude toward himself, he may have a low self-concept even though his statement might not be true on objective measures. But you must take it seriously, for children have a way of making their low opinions come true. On the other hand, he may be saying actually: "I am doing something I know is wrong. Please help me stop." For example, perhaps he is involved in a gang that is shoplifting during lunch hour. In any case, it will not help to pass off such a remark with something like, "Don't be silly, of course you're a good boy."

The frequently occurring problems in caring for foster children that have been discussed in this chapter are not equally serious for the welfare of the child, and it will be helpful to keep your sense of proportion. Other foster parents, as well as the caseworker, are a good source of help and encouragement, and a sense of humor will make life easier for all as you help your child with his difficulties.

# 4

# Discipline

As a general rule, when we talk about discipline and children we really mean punishment or correction. We speak of "disciplining" the child after we administer a spanking or a scolding. Let's begin this chapter by broadening our definition.

Discipline covers all the methods used to train the child in self-control and loving obedience to a standard that considers both his needs and the needs of others. We assume that parents have both a right and duty to set such a standard, to live by it themselves, and to teach, reward, correct, punish and otherwise supervise the child. I assume the parents will do this in such a way that the child can and will undertake more and more responsibility for his own discipline as he grows older.

To start this chapter on what to some may seem a negative note: I believe that every foster parent should renounce the use of physical force directed against a child. Much of what you learn about foster children as you care for them will convince you that renouncing physical force is right, but there will be times in your experiences with a child when only your promise to yourself will prevent you from giving a "well-deserved spanking."

But why not use physical force—spank, slap, shake, etc.?

Number One. It won't work! Many foster children have regularly experienced more physical beating than could possibly be tolerated in your home—more than a couple of slaps on the bottom that might clear the air and reinforce the point that you mean business. A child who has been spanked hard and frequently for offenses great and small will be but briefly, if at all, impressed by your spanking. So having spanked, you will face "What do I do now?" Why not look for alternatives before the spanking?

Number Two. It will alter the way you feel about the child. I am convinced that feelings follow behavior. You will find yourself loving more and more a child you hug and cuddle. With the newborn infant you spend months in which you hug and caress your baby before you even think of such things as spanking him. If the order is reversed and you frequently spank your new foster child in the hope of making him lovable, you are very likely to begin disliking him. No doubt you can justify your dislike and spanking on the basis of his behavior. Are you willing to consider the idea that it is your behavior you dislike too, and that you would like the child out of the way so he doesn't bring out this behavior in you? You and your child need all the positive feelings you can muster if your parent-child relationship is going to meet his needs. The positive feelings have to start with you. So hug him, don't hit him.

Number Three. It will motivate—it will *force*—you to find alternate methods of control. You will have to search for ways to handle the child's behavior. He will have to be kept out of the street, he does have to leave the dishwasher controls alone, he cannot wreck an older child's model plane, he must not swing out the upstairs window. It will test your patience and your ingenuity to find alternative methods, but you can find them. I am going to point out some general ideas and give some illustrations. The thousand and one variations will be up to you. Analyze incidents, read books, think hard about the problem.

Number Four. Not only is there a limit on how much force you can use (and it may not be enough to get the job done, as I mentioned); there is also a time limit. You are attemping to teach this child how to live with himself and others, and the principles you are instilling must last him a lifetime. Unless you are willing to surrender the child to jail when he leaves your home, he has to learn to live acceptably without the fear of a stick over him. Granted, the fear of consequences may be a useful means of control, often built right into a situation. That is not what I am talking about. I mean that at 6 or 12 or 18 or 21, the child will have to act for reasons other than the fear of a physical punishment. So why not use methods that do not have to be abandoned, but that can be worked into the child's own control pattern? You certainly do not want him to grow up beating himself.

Number Five. If the child came to you abused, he has almost certainly been mixed up emotionally to the point where he unintentionally provokes attacks upon himself. Perhaps to him receiving a beating is better than being ignored. In many cases one goal of foster care is to prepare the child to return home. Primarily it will be someone else's job to seek the changes in the own-family home that will break up the abuse cycle. It is part of your opportunity to help the child change so that he does not expect or provoke physical abuse. I think it is especially important to the child that he never be hurt deliberately by you. Teach him to respond to verbal instructions, try to learn the things that especially annoy the abusing parent and see if you can break up some of those action-reaction patterns. Don't reinforce them by continuing the same methods, modified in force though they may be.

As to an approach to discipline, my first suggestion is that you *arrange to get acquainted.* In our home we have a large, well-lighted basement room with indestructible indoor-outdoor carpet. There is a small, bare bathroom that meets functional needs only. Everything in the basement is washable except the television! In a small room are toys that can be kept out of sight or brought out as needed. There are a few pieces of old furniture, some cushions and pillows, a set of kitchen cabinets.

In that basement I get acquainted with a new child. I iron or sew or type—and watch. The tasks I work on tolerate many interruptions. There are a minimum number of dangers to say "no" to, few things to break, no valuable knickknacks or older children's belongings to cause tearful encounters. In that functional setting where I can be calm about it, I find out just how toilet-trained this child is. There are riding toys and rocking horses and play people and blocks. There are trucks and doll babies. These come out slowly as I learn what he can handle and what he likes. After a few days I know much more about this child than I can learn in weeks of usual household routine and with much less wear and tear on the whole family and the house. The family joins us in the basement for meals and when they are home and free. One of the girls may take a child outside or to her room while I get supper. For those few days I avoid taking on outside responsibilities, simplify the household chores and concentrate on kids. Our own preschooler is in the basement getting acquainted too.

If at all possible, try to set up some such arrangement in your home. A sunporch, an extra bedroom, seldom-used formal dining room perhaps could be converted into such a place. It should be as roomy as possible, cheerful and comfortable (so you would want to spend hours on end there), indestructible and self-contained as possible. You have to be there most of the time, and you must have useful things to do yourself. Primarily you are there as an observer, not a playmate. Set up the situation to cause the least possible negative interference from you and the utmost in pleasant experiences for the child. At best, he's been through a lot in the last few days. Give him a chance to relax and get used to you and his new home. Gradually he will be ready to be incorporated more fully into the family. You will have avoided getting a lot of negative interactions going before you know what you are doing.

As you get to know him, begin to *put some structure in his life.* You may have adopted a life style that involves popping into the car on 30 minutes' notice to spend the weekend with a favorite set of cousins in the country. Fine. That particular idea is one we use. But not when we have a new foster child. I think most young children benefit from established times for going to bed, getting up, and napping. They need to eat on schedule and get some regular playtime outside except in bad weather. Later you will learn just how much irregularity a particular child can tolerate well. Maybe he won't mind missing a nap or waiting for dinner. But at first, give him the benefit of the routine. A hungry or tired child cannot respond his best and often gets into trouble or has an accident.

Sticking to schedule also will help you. Caring for a preschool child is physically hard work. You may spend an extra hour getting one to bed—and be up with him 3 hours later just as you thought you were going to bed. So if you can get him to nap on schedule, you may get a much-needed rest. Tired mothers trying to get an already overdue meal onto the table don't have much energy or patience to cope with misbehavior. Give yourself a chance to be at your best as you learn to deal with this child.

**Listen to the child.** I have a faculty for sitting down with a book or magazine and shutting out the world, and I've done it since childhood. It's great for studying and for passing the time in doctors' offices. But this ability makes life difficult for small children. How many times a dish has been broken or a sister's hair pulled in a desperate attempt to get Mother's attention, I can only guess. But I have observed that almost everyone from time to time uses some method to shut out people. Children under 5 aren't skillful at getting around this but they will get through to you somehow. Try to make getting through easier. During the time you are responsible for children, really "be there" for them. Try to hear what is asked of you the first time; don't interrupt their efforts to tell you. Of course you can't spend your whole time listening to children, and they won't want you to. You may have to get "listening" across to others too. There will be more or less deliberate mayhem in the basement if you spend an hour in coffee talk with a neighbor and ignore the warning signals from below.

**Act to break up cycles of misbehavior.** Think of a morning that got off to a bad start. You forgot you needed the car to take one of the children to the dentist later in the morning, so you raced around and piled everyone in the car to drive Dad to work. All that "hurry up and get dressed" got Jimmy (who's the slow type) into a bad frame of mind and yours wasn't much better. You delivered Dad and on the way back into the house Jimmy spied his trike and wanted to stay out and play. Under his jacket was his pajama top, so you said "No" pretty abruptly without explaining. Jimmy wailed and you grabbed his arm and tried to make it through the door with Susie in front of you, the dog bounding at you and Jimmy screaming at the top of his lungs. You got the key in the door, meanwhile spilling half the purse contents. Now you are in the house and you see that no one thought to clear up the breakfast dishes or even put the milk away. Susie, who has been feeling a bit smug because Jimmy has been catching it while she has been "good," now decides to rub it into Jimmy a bit and gets punched in the stomach. And away we go!

Unless you take two deep breaths and get things under control you are in for a long morning. So what do you do? This is where I believe previously thought-out commitments make a difference. If you have a passionate thing about getting the dishes done, I suppose you will have to dump the kids in a room somewhere and tackle the dishes. But if you have previously decided that a crying child is more important than dirty dishes, those dishes won't bother you while you try to help the children get back on key. If you had previously decided that the children should be clean and warm but not necessarily fashionable, you would have been free to say "Yes" instead of "No" to Jimmy's request to ride his tricycle a while. An explanation later that he had to come in and get a shirt on for a trip to the dentist would probably have struck him as reasonable. A big family calendar where everyone jots down and checks on dentist trips, school plays, parties, etc., would have been a great help earlier in the morning. Even with a family calendar you'll forget things—but not so often.

You may be thinking, "Anyone can tell me afterward what I should have done." Right. You can even tell yourself what you should have done, and I am suggesting you do just that. When you have a morning when things get out of hand, try to find time to think it through to see what could have been done. Look for patterns in behavior of all those involved. That puts you in a position to take corrective steps before you have the next go-round.

**Be flexible.** Having talked about schedules and order, I now want to talk about the need to bend your ways to the ways of the foster child. We have three daughters in our household. Don and I decided long ago that trying to "treat each one alike" was a waste of time. The girls are not alike and they never have been. Shirley is in perpetual motion. She loves to read, but even then a foot is waving or a toe tapping somewhere. Ruth loves people *and* privacy and she meets those needs her own way. As a primary school child she would come tearing home from a highly social day at school, give me a quick rundown on the details while she changed clothes, and then head for at least an hour of hard solitary play outside before she was ready for people again. Linda cried easily—big tears rolled down her cheeks. Grandma usually melted before them just as she had melted before Daddy's tears when he was a little boy. I could go on and on.

The point is that from living with our children, we know fairly well what a behavior means to them and we try not to read into it something that fits ourselves or one of the other children. Because perpetual-motion Shirley has difficulty relaxing and going to sleep, she has a fixed bedtime to help her on school nights. Ruth prefers to get all her work done and sleep until the last minute in the morning; Linda finds she can get a fresh start on a difficult math assignment if she gets up at 6 o'clock. As soon and as much as possible, we have tried to make the children responsible for their own personal schedules, within the framework of the family schedule. That means that everyone comes to the table at the regular times, but it doesn't mean all lights out at 10 p.m.

The foster child may have lived in a helterskelter style. Things that seem important to you may not mean a thing to him. Try to go slowly in changing him to fit you. The battles may not be worth it—perhaps your life would be more interesting if you changed your ideas a bit to fit his. Jeff doesn't like to wear shoes. He never did and it took me a while to figure out the reason. They hurt. His feet are exceptionally wide and short, and he was over 4 before he had a pair of shoes he thought were comfortable. So mostly he goes barefoot winter and summer. I suppose he will have to wear shoes to school but I have noticed a fair number in sock feet at our grade school, so perhaps he and his teacher can compromise.

Save your energy for matters that are important to the child's wellbeing in the long haul and don't be drawn into daily hassles about such things as whether he keeps his shoes on.

**Be consistent.** I don't mean to confuse you and contradict myself by saying "Be flexible" and "Be consistent." Most of the foster children who have come to us have lived with parents who have problems. Sometimes these parents have tried to do the best they could with the children. But from the child's point of view, he has been living in a situation where he did not know what to expect next. One day he may have to dress himself in short order and depart with mother to the babysitter before breakfast. The next day may be mother's day off and he and little sister may wander around the house getting into things until 11 o'clock, while mother sleeps in. When she gets up, surveys the damage and faces the prospect of getting a week of housework done in what remains of her day off, the roof may fall in on the kids. Or she may decide to forget the whole thing and take the kids and herself to visit a girlfriend in a similar situation. Time and again a child may find himself getting spanked hard for something his mother was too tired or busy to notice an hour before.

You need a clear idea of your expectations for a child and a consistency (not rigidity) in helping him meet those expectations. Then he won't have to keep testing you to see what you want, and many misbehaviors will be avoided.

**Talk to the child.** Even very young children are able to understand more words than they can use. It is possible that many routines, pieces of equipment and procedures in your home are totally new to the child. In his natural exploration he may hurt himself or appear destructive and ruinous to your things. Try to look at what you are doing with him, to him, before him, from his point of view and explore it with him verbally and manually if possible. Help him understand how things work and what the dangers are. Have you watched a thoughtful doctor examine a child for the first time? Ours always explains as he goes, telling the child what he is doing, commenting on the instruments, using words to allay the fears of the child over this strange procedure. Especially at first, you can avoid misbehavior born out of fear or curiosity if you explain, explain—and listen to his questions.

**Set standards.** In all the discussion of problems and discipline, I have implied that there should be considerable leeway in your enforcement of standards on the children in the early days of adjustment. I do not mean that this can continue indefinitely. You will have to work toward a goal of one set of standards to be applied in a flexible way to all members of the family. A foster child cannot be permitted to throw food at the table without consequences when your own child would be sent from the table to his room. If your child would lose bike-riding privileges for leaving the bike lying on the sidewalk, a foster child will have to lose them too. You should see that your foster child lives by the normal standards of your family. Of course you cannot coerce his inner acceptance of these, but you can begin to build behavior patterns.

If you do not try, you will place yourself, your own children, and the foster child in a set of impossible positions. First of all, your children will rightfully resent two sets of behavior standards. They may properly conclude that the expectations can't be so important, or you would be more consistent about making them stick for this new member of the family. Second, I think you will tend to resent the foster child's behavior and take it out on him somehow. His bad manners or his rudeness or disobedience will annoy you and you will be ashamed of your tolerance of it even if you tolerate it under the guise of "being understanding." Last, the foster child may come to feel that he is getting gypped. You have agreed to be his parent, yet you are not behaving toward him as toward your own children. And his behavior may get worse and worse, as he tries to determine whether you care enough about him to limit him and to help him correct his behavior.

To summarize: Get acquainted with your foster child, put some structure into his life (and yours if necessary), listen to the child, act to break up cycles of misbehavior, be flexible, be consistent, talk to the child, and set standards.

Keep in mind that these principles are to be applied so that the number of misbehaviors is reduced to a minimum. I believe that if you deal with a child in such a manner from babyhood, most days you and the child will get along well together. You will be making progress toward your goal of a self-disciplined person.

However, the chances are this child whom you are now parenting has had to adapt his behavior to some pretty confusing surroundings. From experience I know that a 2-year-old can look at you with pure fury and spit in your face and a 4-year-old may pull your cat's tail every chance he gets. You can explain that it hurts and he'll pull with extra glee. You can understand in a general way the reasons behind such behavior, but your cat must be protected and the spitting must stop before it's your neighbor's face.

I remember the first time I was spit at by a foster child. I was on my knees at her face level trying to find out what she was screaming about. When she spit I took her shoulders and told her firmly, "Jeanie, you must not spit at the Mommy in this house." She promptly urinated, creating a puddle at my knees. I went for the mop and considered that round lost.

Before we get too specific about corrective methods, let us admit that we are going to lose quite a few rounds. Before much progress is seen, a warm, affectionate basis for interaction must be established with the child. The most effective method of obtaining desired behavior from a child is to have the doing of it make him feel good. Small children feel good when they feel loved. They will imitate the behavior of loving parents. That love won't just "happen." You must decide to love him and set about acting toward him in loving ways. Let me give an example.

Mike has just watched out of the corner of his eye while you spent 20 minutes feeding the baby. You enjoyed it and so did the baby. After a couple of rather tentative attempts to get some attention, Mike went off to the playroom and began writing on the walls. When you discover this you remark rather sternly-sadly in the approved modern manner

"Mother doesn't like Mike to write on the walls. That wasn't nice of Mike." Mike couldn't care less. He is already pretty sure Mike isn't liked as much as that baby upstairs anyway, so what does he have to lose?

Most mothers reading this book would have recognized Mike's feelings, spent some extra time with him reassuring him of his special place. He could be corrected for the scribbling. Mike would feel good again and the scribbling probably would not be repeated at the next feeding time. But withdrawal of affection or approval cannot have any positive meaning for a child who is not convinced underneath his temporary discomfort that he already has affection and approval.

**Built on an established basis of affection,** here are some methods I have found will work at least some of the time.

**A clear, verbal scolding and explanation of what was wrong with what he did.** This should be short, not a long harangue. It should cover only the particular incident under reprimand. It is not fair to drag in yesterday's misdeeds. The scolding should refer to the deed only, not to the child's character. Try to speak calmly, plainly and firmly and try to have the child's full attention.

Example: "John, you pulled the cat's tail. That hurts the cat and you are not to do that."

Not: "John, that is the fourteenth time today I have seen you pull that cat's tail and I'm getting plenty sick and tired of it. The next time I see you mauling that cat you're going to catch it. How would you like to have your tail pulled? Now get out of here and leave that poor cat alone." And on and on if you happen to notice that his attention was wandering the first time you said it.

**A few minutes' isolation.** Some children who are absolutely unmoved by a scolding get the point swiftly that you are displeased when you withdraw yourself physically from them. I used to put Ruth in her room alone when she had temper tantrums at age 3. Not only did she calm down more rapidly than by any other method we tried, but she began to go there on her own when she felt furious. We might slip in a few minutes later to find her fast asleep, or more likely, looking at a book or dressing dolls.

You should not place a small child in his room for long periods or sit him on a chair for an hour. Time beyond 5 to 10 minutes is pretty meaningless to a small child. He probably will forget why he was there and may even plot new mischief. After a time appropriate to the child's age (not to the seriousness of the misbehavior) has passed, repeat verbally the behavior you want, and give him some hugging and verbal expressions of affection.

Some young children have adopted the pattern of falling into a fantasy world whenever life around becomes unpleasant and outside stimulation stops. I would not use the isolation method with such children.

**Remove the source of temptation temporarily.** If you have given plain instructions that a ball is not to be thrown at the lights but rolled on the floor, and the child continues to throw it, put the ball up, saying as you do something like, "I asked you to roll the ball on the floor. You may have it back to play with it that way." Try to find a chance to take him outside where he can test his skill at heaving the ball at a tree trunk or some other likely target. Again, keep in mind the child's short memory. If you put the ball up for a week he will forget why it disappeared.

Some household objects that frequently cause problems may be handled in a similar way, by removing the object if possible. I came home one night at 9 o'clock to the announcement that not a drain in the house was working. Nine persons, including two in diapers, and not a working toilet. Thanks to the kind of emergency service one can still get in a small town, we went to bed with the main drain open again. I was less experienced then, and had spent 2 days trying to convince a 4-year-old to leave the drain cover alone. I didn't know that every time I heard the telltale clank another small toy was on its way to the ocean. Somewhere along the line the shipment got snagged on tree roots. And late that night after Rotor Rooter left, Don had the electric drill out putting that drain cover permanently in place. It may be cheaper, simpler, and easier on everybody involved to child-proof your house. Especially if you expect to have a succession of small children, the extra trouble of adding a lock or moving a switch higher will be worth it.

**Provide for short attention span.** From your own experience with children you know that there is great individual difference in the length of time a child can pay attention to one activity. One 4-year-old will sit quietly most of the way through "Sesame Street" or play for nearly an hour building block towers. Another child of the same chronological age finds it hard to listen to a 5-minute picture story.

It is not your task to keep providing new and interesting activities. He'll run you ragged and he does have to learn to entertain himself. But do provide a variety of things for him to do and don't insist that he finish one block tower before he starts riding his horse. If you do he may then more or less casually heave a block at the lamp. He just isn't interested in towers any more. If he is a child who always wants whatever his playmate is currently playing with, you may have to separate him physically, with toys of his own. In the long run I think you will be sorry if you let yourself be drawn into "I had it first" quarrels. Time and patience tend to solve this problem, and you will find the child playing without help from you for longer periods of time.

**Gear his activities to his style.** You would like your children to enjoy a story, be creative with play materials, enjoy a good romp in the outdoors and play imaginatively with toys. But it is unrealistic to think that any one child is going to have all of these interests. If you happen to like books and keep forcing them on a child who hasn't learned to care about them he probably will tear them. A child who doesn't enjoy playing outside with other children may repeatedly run into the street —especially if the penalty is 30 minutes inside. If your foster child is continually misbehaving in the same way, try to figure out whether he is bored or unhappy with the activity he is engaged in at the time.

**Teach him how to play.** What looks like carelessness with toys or meanness with other children may actually be inexperience. Enlist help from older children to teach the child simple games. Take time to be certain he knows what you mean by "share" or "take turns."

We have taught the concept of sharing by letting a child be "passer-outer" of treats. Without risk on his part he has a chance to share what he has. They are your cookies and he has seen there are more where these came from. He will enjoy the pleasant feeling of importance he has and the pleasure he is giving. He will progress from being sure everyone got one of *your* cookies to assuming quite naturally that it is fun to share what is his. Sound too good to be true? It really will work. On the other hand, I've found that forced sharing results in little but hard feelings. Once again, division of toys and separation of the children may be necessary. I explain as I separate the children that they may have the fun of playing together again when they stop fighting over the toys.

**Let him feel consequences.** Unless there is serious danger involved, let the child test and learn for himself the consequences of breaking rules. At the same time, avoid threats. "If you play with the TV switch, I'm going to turn it off" may seem like fair warning at the time. But the child may feel an irresistible urge to give the knob one last twist just to test the situation. Now you have to turn the TV off, he is miserable, and you really didn't want to have to take away his beloved Mr. Rogers. I try to say something like, "Leave the TV alone so we can all hear Mr. Rogers." I hope it sounds reasonable to him and is enough to keep his hands off the TV. If he continues to twirl knobs, I turn the TV off and comment that we will try to listen tomorrow. So what is the difference? He still lost his program. But he didn't give you that edgy impression that he was defying you to see what happens *in you.* The action and the consequences remain associated with the TV.

**Don't make a test case out of a minor incident.** You are deeply concerned about the welfare of this child, and you know that these early years of training are important. You are tempted to say to yourself,

"But he has to learn to get along with people" when the incident was a simple hairpulling. Or "What will happen to him if he doesn't learn to respect and obey me," when he climbed out of bed at nap time. Right now he has to stop pulling hair and take his nap. Try not to read complex emotions and long-term consequences into simple misdeeds.

**How to analyze a child's misbehavior.** Several times in this chapter I have proposed mentally stepping aside and sizing up the situation. Now I'd like to suggest a method for analyzing incidents of child misbehavior.

We have to clarify some assumptions before we spell out the details. First of all, the method assumes that the behavior of this child makes sense; that what he is doing can be understood, and that what you know about other children can be used in understanding this child. The child's behavior is not occurring in an irrational vacuum.

The second assumption is that you can come to understand yourself better, and that this is necessary to understanding the child. The behavior of a child brings about changes in the parent. Our reactions and feelings are part of the situation too and we need to be aware of them and understand them.

The third assumption is that "understanding" is a continuing process, not a place we arrive. We will never completely understand the child; but we are continually trying to take into account the forces that make him act the way he does (and make us act as we do).

The core of the method is the careful observation of a behavior for later analysis. It helps to write down your observations, if possible. It is of course unrealistic to think a mother can stop to write a couple of paragraphs when she is trying to peel apart two fighting boys or comfort a little girl whose favorite doll just lost an arm in the hands of her brother. But perhaps you can write the essentials down in your own shorthand later. Be sure to date and time the incident. Try to include the following as you observe and record.

1. **What set him off?** What triggered this incident? What was happening just before?

2. **What happened?** Be objective and nonjudgmental in your description?

3. **What happened afterward?** What did you do? What did other people do? What did he do? What did the environment do?

Step one may be a bit difficult—often you arrive on the scene after the dish is broken or the hairpulling has begun. It won't be very useful to question the child! Instead, pick incidents to analyze where you do know pretty accurately the first phase.

Step two involves a description of the incident. Be objective in that you describe what you saw happen, not what you think happened. But also try to give a sense of the flavor of the situation. How something is said is just as important as what was said, but be as accurate and noninterpretative as you can. Describe *all* that happened. Note all the persons on hand and what they did. Also, be nonjudgmental. Of course, it is your responsibility to make judgments and act accordingly. But in your record try to stick to facts. "He tore her doll's arm out of spite" may be true, but once you have made and recorded that judgment it is harder to consider the possibility that he acted for some other reason. We are writing and analyzing to gain understanding, so don't close the door to possible interpretations of his behavior at this point.

What happened afterward? In your first efforts, you may be surprised to find how hard it is to include all that was done, said, or just happened after the behavior occurred. This is important because somewhere in that bundle of happenings was the thing that rewarded the child's behavior, and caused it or similar behavior to be repeated. Something that made it "worth it" to the child. After you have carefully recorded a number of such incidents, that reward may stand out like a sore thumb and you will be in a position to act on your new knowledge.

Some children come to value what are called socially unacceptable rewards. That is, something we would not regard as a reward has positive meaning to this particular child in certain situations. A really mixed-up child may prefer such rewards much of the time. The child may enjoy punishing himself or others, or may enjoy being punished in some way. Talk with him about his behavior and feelings. You have a tremendous handle on the situation when a child has language—use it. Explain that he would feel good if he smiled and handed the toy to his friend. Help him do just that with smiles and encouragement and a smile on your own face. Say, "Don't you feel good when you smile and Jimmy smiles at you." Skeptical? Try it.

After you have analyzed the child's behavior, use your imagination to try to interrupt and change the patterns you see. Remember that new patterns are easier to interrupt and change than well-established habits.

**The child who does not improve.** It is necessary to comment about the difficult child who does not appear to change though you are trying to carry out the ideas and principles suggested in this chapter. He has you going in circles, the whole family is beginning to resent the amount of time and energy his problems require, and you feel you haven't even won his notice, let alone his affection.

First, do you feel an affectionate concern for this particular child? No guilt involved here—just an honest evaluation of how you feel about him. Perhaps you would have to say, "Well, yes, I like him, but he just asks more of me than I have to give." Or, "No. Frankly, I haven't learned to like him very much. He doesn't seem to respond to me as a parent at all and I'm tired of the constant strain of trying to get through to him."

Next, take the matter to the child's caseworker. Of course no foster child should be moved for superficial reasons. But you will not be doing him a favor by keeping him in an atmosphere of failure. Explain honestly and openly what has been going on between you and the child and how you feel about the situation. Make some notes ahead of time, even if you don't use them. You will be clearer in your mind and make more sense to the caseworker. The evaluation and conference should be a husband-wife project, even if only one of you ends up doing the talking.

Ask the caseworker to arrange for a professional evaluation of the child. There may be a real learning disability. You have done the best you could and it is time to learn whether this child has an emotional development problem. Not all children recover easily from harsh early experiences. Don't be defensive or embarrassed—ask for help. The professional child worker may be able to help you learn to help this child. He may be able to help you get at the roots of difficulty in the child. He may recommend a different placement where there are fewer siblings or a mother with more time. For the sake of the child's future, do what you can to get him in a situation where he is behaving well with a family, either yours or some other. If the child is moved, don't take it as a personal failure but as a positive action to improve the quality of living for you and your family and for him. And ask for another foster child as soon as you have had a rest.

Occasionally foster parents find themselves in a difficult bind, especially with older foster children in counseling. They have asked for help, but after a few sessions with the child, the counselor decides it is the foster family that needs to change to fit the child. At this point you will have to make a decision. If you believe you are right in what you are requiring of the child, you will have to stick to your position as parents in the home. The child's behavior must change or he must be moved. But please, exhaust all the possibilities before taking this drastic step. The older the child, the more likely he is to take his problems into the new home, where they may prove to be just as hard on the new family. Too often foster teenage children undergo a series of moves from family to family, with no chance to develop the affectionate ties that might enable them to want to please anyone.

*THE AGENCY*

# 5

# The Job of the Caseworker

The link between you and the agency that placed your foster child is the caseworker. I use "her" for the caseworker since most often the child welfare worker who visits your home is a woman. Many people involved in child welfare programs would welcome changes that would make it possible to have more men in the field, but we have known only one male caseworker.

The caseworker's job is defined for her by the policies and regulations of the agency. The agency in turn is governed by state and national laws. Actions that may seem unnecessary or unwise to you may be dictated by such regulations and not the preference of the worker. If a summary of her responsibilities is available, ask for a copy. This section is written to reflect her position as caseworker in relation to you as foster parent. It is not intended to cover other aspects of her work, and some are not even mentioned. Our Foster Parents Association includes in its handbook a list of the caseworker's responsibilities in relation to the foster parent.* In general, she has five principal duties. The caseworker keeps track of how the child is doing in the foster home, she serves as your formal contact with the agency for technical purposes, she keeps official records, she maintains contact with the own parents, and she helps you to deal with the child living with you. In some agencies these duties are divided among a team of workers.

Since the agency retains responsibility for the child and delegates the care to you, the caseworker will be keeping track of the welfare of

---

* See Appendix.

the child. She should check to see how you are doing, make inquiries about the child, be concerned with all aspects of his development. She should know the questions to ask and you should expect her to ask them and give her full answers. No responsible foster parent should consider such activity on the caseworker's part "snooping."

She also will serve as your contact with the agency. If you need permission to take the child out of state, need a letter of authorization for special services, or have technical questions of any kind, she is the person to call. Generally she will provide you with phone numbers and names for emergency use.

She keeps official records regarding the child. The official records are important. In a sense they are the only permanent element in the situation. The foster child may move from your home, the caseworker may retire, the parents may move to another state. The records remain in the file and upon the basis of information in them, decisions regarding the child will be made. The records should be accurate, and it will help if you are certain that anything you tell the caseworker for the record is factual and complete.

In addition to serving you and the child, the caseworker may act as the contact between the parents and the agency. She may have responsibility for obtaining services they need, especially placing them in contact with those that will help the parents get ready to resume care of their child. She will help to arrange visits within the guidelines the court or agency has set for the child. She may even pick the child up for such visits or accompany the parents to your home. She is the primary person who is getting to know the situation, problems, strengths and weaknesses of the parents, as you are the primary person who is getting to know the child.

As a fifth area of responsibility, the caseworker is available to help you solve problems and to answer your questions. It is not an imposition to ask for help. You will never reach the point where you know all there is to know about caring for foster children, and the caseworker is continuously involved in training you to do the job better. As you attempt to help a particular child, you will be learning together.

Generally, the caseworker has been formally educated in social work. As a rule, part of this education has been some form of inservice training program. There are rules governing the care of foster children and the help given to their families. Since the rules are constantly changing, she has learned where to find out what she needs to know about the technical aspects of her work. There is a body of law in foster care, and she and her supervisor have access to a lawyer when this kind of advice is necessary.

Another aspect of her education has been general schooling in principles of social welfare. She may have specialized in child care or some other field, since her job requires not only skill with children, but knowledge of how to help other age groups. Much can be learned from books, and she has had considerable opportunity to read and to discuss general principles with others. This enables her to bring to your problems some degree of general wisdom.

A good caseworker has solid background in knowledge, is growing through her experiences, and has insight and empathy with people. On the other hand, she is no magician. We have a tendency to invest professionals with an aura of magic. We may overvalue their advice or take it too literally, even when it is against all common sense. She will prove to be less than perfect and if you expect perfection you will be disappointed. Such an expectation is hardly fair to her.

The caseworker is dependent upon you for the facts, opinions and impressions upon which she bases decisions regarding the child. If you want to get significant help from her you will have to be accurate and fair in your observations about the child and be willing to share them with your caseworker. Remember that your feelings about the facts are important. You also must trust her enough to communicate them.

How often will she or should she visit? It is almost a cliché that caseworkers are overloaded. That it has been said so often does not make it less true, and she simply cannot waste time. Usually there is not enough time to do all she would like to do even with the most careful budgeting of her hours. How much time she spends with you is governed somewhat by how much time she can spare.

The number and types of visits will be partly determined by the individual case situation. A child may be placed in foster care for a few weeks while his mother has an operation and makes a recovery. Another child may be with you awaiting an opening in a special school or institution. Perhaps in neither of these cases would much supervision be required. Usually in a long-term placement there would be frequent visits during an early adjustment period. The visits would become less frequent when all of you had learned to think of the foster child as integrated into your family.

A new foster home may expect a few more visits than one that has been operating long enough for mutual confidence to have developed between the agency staff and the foster parents.

In any case, if you feel you need to talk, telephone your caseworker. A visit can be arranged at her office or your home, probably immediately if the matter is urgent, a little later if it can wait. If you don't hear from your caseworker, she is assuming that all is going well.

Because your caseworker is just as human as you are, she also may become discouraged or seem indifferent at times. This should not surprise you. Remember that you see only a small part of her work. She has to live with the knowledge that in spite of her best efforts, many of the situations in her caseload can be improved only marginally. For every "happy ending" to a child's story there are many sad ones. The solutions represent coming to terms with the world we have. Often a caseworker will learn in trying to help a family that she is dealing with a second-generation problem. Some other agency did the best it could years before, yet now a former foster child has to have a child placed in foster care.

The best caseworkers face these periods of discouragement, recognize their disappointments—and keep trying. If they cannot do this, they tend to leave the field. Occasionally, I suppose, one stays and goes through the motions, but I have never met such a social worker.

If life is going well for your child and the caseworker has helped you, let her know. She has need of your encouragement and will appreciate it.

# 6

# Sharing Responsibility

Working with the caseworker is a matter of sharing responsibility. In practice it is difficult to draw the line between your responsibility and that of the agency. You must work together for the welfare of the child. How much you do and how much the agency does cannot be determined according to a formulation supplied by a third party. It is worked out case by case.

One area of shared responsibility is in planning for the child. Goals for his development while he is in foster care are important. The child should not be in some sort of holding pattern while waiting for the adult world around him to make up its mind about his future. He needs the opportunities of any other child. If he has been hurt by past experiences, the measures necessary to overcome this should be started promptly. That he is in foster care should not mean he cannot get started on music lessons or have his teeth straightened at the time most of his classmates do. A lot of these things depend on your initiative. You have to think about goals and plans for him and then ask your caseworker to help you evaluate them and work out the technical aspects of effecting them.

Another type of planning is more exclusively up to the initiative of the caseworker. She must obtain the facts and make judgments as to the future care of the foster child. Can he and should he be adopted? Can his own home be readied for his return? How soon? Your part in this planning is to furnish the caseworker with accurate information about the child. You may have some opinions, too, about what would be good for him on a long-term basis. You have the right to participate in this planning on behalf of the child, and you probably will be asked to.

At this point the caseworker is particularly interested in knowing all the things about the child that will help her place him in the best possible situation for him. You may have talked about the child's personality or special gifts from time to time, but this will be the time to summarize and reevaluate. If the child is old enough to have an opinion, what would he like to have happen next? Perhaps you have an idea of what he wants though he hasn't dared express it openly. In the face of the rights of the child's own parents, the policies of public officials, the economics of the situation, and other factors, try to be an informed and loving advocate of the child. Speak for him, and help him make his own needs known. The caseworker will appreciate your openness.

You cannot expect that what you think should happen is always going to be the solution adopted. For instance, Kenny had been with us several months and was ready to be placed for adoption. This decision had been arrived at in the agency staff and under supervision of the courts and although we knew what was happening, we were not involved in this aspect of the work. This is normal procedure. Now a new caseworker was seeking a suitable adoptive home for him, and came to talk about Kenny's needs. We talked at some length about Kenny, his personality, his development during foster care, the kind of care he required, and our progress toward the goals we had in mind for him. Then she told me about the home where she expected to place him. It seemed totally wrong. I did not see how the placement could possibly be successful, and we talked about that too. In the end she went ahead with the placement. I cannot resist telling you that the placement did not work, because I want to encourage you to share your opinions with the caseworker. You are the amateur in the picture, but you probably know more about your foster child than anyone else does. My information did help in the second placement.

This illustrates how the responsibility is shared. It was my job to give her a clear picture of Kenny and his needs, and state my opinion that the needs would not be met in the home she had described. It was her responsibility to assess what I told her and the homes that were available, and make the decision.

This brings us to the matter of conflict in your relationship with the caseworker. There is room for disagreement over the best way to handle the shared responsibility for the child. Disagreement can grow into conflict. Whether that conflict is openly expressed and openly dealt with makes a great deal of difference. Conflict need not be destructive. It helps to know some areas where you can expect to disagree sometimes.

Occasionally there is conflict over discipline and privileges. Ordinarily the caseworker does not second-guess the foster parents in the day-to-day handling of the child. If the child cannot adjust without damage to the style and methods of the family, he will probably be moved. But moving a child is hard on him, and his behavior may be designed to test whether you care enough about him to put up with what he sees other children getting away with, or perhaps whether you care enough to make him stop. The caseworker may try to mediate your differences. If she is tactless or you are defensive, you may wind up with a serious difference. It is to be hoped that there is a procedure in your agency for handling disagreements between agency representatives and foster parents, and that both of you use it. It is not your pride or the caseworker's rightness that is at stake. The child's life is the prize. As mentioned in connection with discipline, many foster children are moved at this point and if they are in their teens, as is likely, the conflict will be renewed in the new home. Unless something special happens it can be downhill all the way. You didn't move your own children out when you got into a disciplinary struggle with them, and I think foster children are entitled to the same permanence in their relationship.

Do you know the expression, "Don't air your dirty linen in public?" It is pretty out of date in the age of automatic laundries and wash and wear, but I haven't learned a new one to replace it. I know of a case where conflict between caseworker and foster parents was permitted to escalate to the point where the child had to be moved. The foster parents then wrote a letter to the local newspaper, airing the grievance to the general public. I am glad to say the agency did not respond to it publicly. The publicity was unfair to a particular child and unfair to the child care program as a whole. We need the respect and help of the general community. No good can come from a one-sided presentation of a dispute to listeners unprepared to do anything constructive about it.

Responsibility is also shared in the area of relations between the child and his parents. The agency may permit parental visits that from your point of view only upset the child. You may expend much effort solving a particular problem, only to find it renewed every time you get the child back after a weekend with his parents. It helps to remember that the caseworker is obligated to keep in mind the welfare of the child, your rights as foster parents, and *the welfare and rights of the parents.* You will gain better understanding if you tell the caseworker how you feel and ask her to explain to you what she is trying to accomplish by actions that are causing problems for you.

The foster parent is pretty much a "nonperson" when it comes to legal responsibility for the child. Under present laws, which vary widely from state to state, it seems unlikely that we will ever avoid all the serious conflicts that arise from this. But you should remember that the child, no matter how long he stays with you is most likely the ward of the court. Do not assume that either you or the child have earned any rights beyond those granted by the law. If you think the child's legal status can or should be changed, work through the agency and its lawyers. Often custody conflicts wind up in courts because parties to a situation drifted along for years, and action that could have been taken to establish firmer legal status for the child was not taken.

**Responsibility for keeping records.** As mentioned, the responsibility for keeping official records concerning the foster child rests with the agency. You do not need to keep track of court hearings, for instance, and you can assume that the caseworker is keeping a running account of developments in the child's total situation. There are some records, however, that are your responsibility, and some that may prove of value and are worth keeping on your own.

Even if you are not given a form to do so, keep a health record for the child. If you receive any details at all concerning immunizations, general health, birth health—anything at all—begin your record by noting these in the clearest form possible. Jot down even those things you are not sure of, and note the uncertainty. Then keep a careful record of all health procedures taken and all illnesses while the child is with you. This should include suspicions regarding allergies and the names of medicines he has taken. Include ongoing information about height and weight.

I emphasize that this record should be clear and complete. The child may have to be moved into a new home. All the things you would be able to tell a doctor in a few minutes must be on paper if the new parent is going to know the things needed. In an emergency, time to contact you may be unavailable.

For your personal use and enjoyment, you will want to keep a record of the time the child spends with you. In journal form I keep a running account of the life of the child. This is also the place to record problems, note special gains, jot down questions that are puzzling you. Then when the caseworker comes, a quick review of your journal reminds you of the things you wanted to talk over with her.

If the child's stay with you will cover more than a few months, start a third kind of record. This record you will be keeping for the child. Into a folder or box of some sort will go the mementos of the part of his childhood spent with you: duplicates of some of the snapshots you take of him, school projects he felt especially proud of, school pictures and report cards, souvenirs of vacations. If he leaves, these go with him to serve as bridges between his life with you and his life in the new home. If he ends up growing up in your home, he has the same kind of junk and record of his growing up as any other child. A sense of where he belongs is important to any child; for a foster child it can be a major consideration. Be sure he doesn't have to say, "I don't have a thing from my childhood." The things you saved are concrete evidence that he lived with you and that you loved him enough to want to save reminders of the time together.

*THE PARENTS*

# 7

## You and the Child's Parents

No aspect of foster care presents a greater challenge to you than your relationship with the child's own parents. Various details in their lives and the life of the child make each situation different, but some of the emotional factors remain fairly constant. How you yourself handle the fact that the child has another set of parents cannot be separated from the welfare of the child for whom you are caring.

The relation begins in some sort of objective fact: The parents are dead; the parents are ill and unable to care for the child; the parents have been judged by courts to be unfit to care for the child. You are entitled to know the facts of the situation and should be trusted to use them wisely in dealing with the child. If the facts are uncertain or unknown, you should know that too.

The relationship between you and the parents is not necessarily an active interaction. I am using the word relationship to cover active interactions and also the set of feelings that develops within you because of your mental image of the parents who are alive somewhere, or who exist as memory in the child.

Let's discuss first some ideas in relation to deceased parents or parents who are believed to be permanently out of the child's life. Such a situation might arise, for example, when a father is divorced and gives consent to a second husband's adoption of his child, who is later placed.

Because the child does not remember the parent or does not talk about the absent parent does not relieve you of responsibility to keep communication open. Of course, you do not want to stir up emotional

61

debris of a settled situation. But in most cases you can make a casual reference such as, "You must have gotten those pretty blue eyes from your mother," or "Did you know your daddy was over six feet tall?" For the child who may want to ask questions and is afraid you do not want him to, this is sufficient opening. It is possible he has no need or desire to talk about the absent parent.

I have a friend who was placed in foster care at 2 and subsequently adopted. She is a happy, wholesome person who loves her adoptive parents dearly. But she told me that she longed many times to ask, "What did my (biological) mother look like?" and similar questions but was afraid her adoptive mother would interpret the questions as reflecting a lack of love for her. Some older children become almost obsessed with a need to know about their biological parents, though when younger, they avoided the subject. These reactions may be ways of avoiding or trying to answer the question, "Who am I?" Foster parents who have kept open communication in the matter of parents are in a much better position to help the child understand his feelings about his own parents, and to help him deal with the primary question.

For many families in our society, death is the unmentionable subject. All parents must help their children come to terms with death. In the death of a natural parent, death has come not to a pet or a squirrel but to a most important person, and your kindest and best-informed help.is needed.

If a parent is not dead, but is completely out of the child's life, matter-of-fact acceptance of this by you will help the child accept it. The child may still grow up feeling he has to go looking for his own parent some day. Whether he does, with all the attendant psychological risk, depends partly on factors you cannot control. But you can be kind and realistic about the situation, and this may help him avoid overvaluing this possible encounter.

The majority of children in foster care have living parents, often in the same community. Your relationship with them may involve getting to know persons you would not be likely to meet in any other way. Their values, life style, and goals for their children may be entirely different from yours. And since families with children in foster care are under stress, the parents may have little inclination or emotional strength to invest in developing a relationship with you. But the fact that you are caring physically for the child means that you will have a mental relationship with them, and probably some contact as well.

Your dealings with the parents (and your foster child's dealings with them) are under the agency's supervision, ordinarily exercised through the caseworker. Depending on the case, the guidelines governing the situation may be set by the courts. Even with the best of intentions, do not try to act on your own in the matter of the child and his parents or you and his parents. It is not your right or responsibility, unless authority is given you in a particular case through the agency. You may do much harm where you meant only good. That does not mean you cannot take the initiative to discuss with the caseworker something you would like to try.

My inclination with some parents, unfortunately, is to forget they exist. Sometimes thinking about them stirs up feelings I don't want to acknowledge in myself. Sometimes I want to think a beautiful child will not have to go back to a place where he was so unhappy. I have to fight that inclination, and so will you for the sake of yourself and the child.

The next few pages cover some ways you can be of help to the parents and consequently to the child.

**Support the efforts of the parent to be a parent.** By your standards a particular mother may be inadequate and it may seem as though she only makes things worse for the child when she acts. But you have to start somewhere. Let me give an example. The parent asks you as she brings the child home to you after a visit, "Does Sue need anything I could get her?" So you think a minute and say, "Well, yes. She could use a dress to wear when the choir at school gives its concert next month. It's supposed to be fairly simple and a pastel color. She takes a size 10 now." Next week the parent brings the dress. It is red dotted swiss, with seven ruffles of lace down the skirt, white collar and cuffs, and is marked "Dry Clean Only."

Your first reaction may be to treat the parent like a not-too-bright teenager. You use the occasion to impress on the parent just how inadequate she is. You say that the dress won't do because it is the wrong color—you told her pastel. You ask her to take it back and get some underwear. (You probably won't get the underwear and I don't blame the mother.) Then you point out to Sue that she doesn't have a new dress for the concert like the other girls because her mother didn't get the right one, even though you told her what Sue needed.

Something like the following is what you should say. You thank her for the dress, let Sue try it on so the mother can see how pretty it looks, and mention that though you aren't sure they are going to wear any red dresses to the concert, there is another occasion coming up when the dress will be just right. You explain to Sue that this is a very good dress and she will be able to wear it only for special occasions because it must be dry-cleaned. But then it's too pretty to wear just any old time anyway. You can comment that the size 10 fits and its lucky her mother was able to judge her size so well.

Do you think the first reaction was extreme and that anyone would know better than to react that way? Not at all. Ask any caseworker and be honest about your own feelings. You will find that the reaction is natural, and must be fought. The principle of accepting what the parent can do now in a way that encourages better performance in the future needs constant, imaginative application.

**Play second fiddle to his own parents.** The next principle calls for unselfishness. If you are doing a proper job of parenting a foster child, the great bulk of his needs is being met by you. But he has one need you cannot meet—he needs to be able to love his parents. This works out differently at different ages, but the need is never absent. You hope his need is met eventually by a corresponding need of his parents to love him, and you do all you can to foster and strengthen love between them.

You should give opportunity for the child and parents to express their love for each other. You may have to listen to bragging about the neat times he has when he is with his own family even when you are in the car making a trip to the zoo because he's never been there. You will have to convey respect and acceptance of his parents. You won't have to point out their weaknesses, but he won't be able to acknowledge them to you or even to himself unless he has confidence that you won't use them to belittle them or him.

No matter how long he lives with you, you must be willing to accept the fact that the child has membership in another family by birth and he may very well prefer, at least at times, to emphasize that membership rather than the voluntary relation of caring he has with you.

Before I give you the wrong impression: I wrote of unselfishness, not martyrdom on your part. Be sensible. If you think about it you know when what is being asked of you is ridiculous or impractical. You and the child are obligated to live in a real world, and so are his parents.

**Don't play games.** You may find yourself in the middle of a disagreement between the parents and the caseworker, which results in conflict between you and the caseworker. You may have been selected by the parent for a role in "Let's You and Him Fight." This complication can develop with all sorts of variations, the most hazardous one being that in which you and the child are doing the fighting. Without being unfair to the minority of successful parents whose children are in foster care for unusual reasons, I think it is helpful to realize that parents often represent a variety of undesirable coping behaviors, including problems in taking responsibility. The best caseworkers seem to have the ability to recognize an attempt to manipulate them, and to stop it without breaking up the caseworker-parent relationship. When the parent cannot manipulate the caseworker, the parent (who may have maintained his distance previously) may attempt to manipulate the foster parent. This is one reason why what you try to offer in help should be discussed with the caseworker. She probably has a lot more experience in offering help in useful ways. I think you should not get involved in the personal or financial affairs of the parent unless the caseworker agrees.

**Be honest with the parents.** Being honest with the parents may be a lot harder than it sounds. For one thing, it means that you cannot enter into the unreal world of planning for the impossible that some parents create. I knew one parent who insisted strongly on each of her infrequent visits that this would be the last, since by next time she would have enough money saved to take the child home. Most of the time she did not even have a job; she was married to a drug addict much older than herself, and was highly dependent upon him and unable to break with him. During visits she would say to her child, "The next time Mommy comes she will take you home with her." I used to remind her gently but firmly of the terms the courts had given her for return of the child. I do not know whether she ever accepted them and worked to recover the child. It was difficult but honest to interrupt her making empty promises to her son.

Being honest does not mean passing judgment or saying everything you think. It does mean that you will not enter into the evasions of the parent or practice them yourself. Nor should you pretend to be the parent's friend and actually be undermining his position with his child.

Of course, when even a small step is taken that may lead to growth in the parent and possible restoration of the family, it should be met with encouragement. Your knowledge that the obstacles are tremendous (if they are) should not be used by you to destroy whatever hope the parent has.

**Support the caseworker-parent relationship.** For various reasons a great deal of distrust and hostility may be directed toward the caseworker by the parents. This can arise out of something specific, such as the fact that the caseworker gave evidence that helped to cause removal of the child. The parent will not stop to consider that the caseworker did not make up the evidence. Or there may be a much more generalized antagonism to welfare and all its parts. The parents' widespread resentment of the conditions of their lives is frequently directed at the agency. Many who receive much help from welfare agencies resent both the need for help and the people through whom it is delivered. The child care worker may be the target of resentment that has little direct connection with her actions.

In this situation, you can help by explaining to the parent the actions the caseworker takes. You may be able to help the parent see that he is blaming the caseworker for actions or results not of her making. Even if the parent has a well-founded gripe, you may be able to show him how to take it to the caseworker and give her a chance to repair the situation. You may be able to convince the parent that caseworkers have rules to follow, and that all concerned have to accomplish their ends within the regulations. The advantages to the parent and her child of working in cooperation with the agency instead of at sword's point can be pointed out. But don't forget you want to increase understanding, not take sides.

Possibly you can also help the caseworker understand the parent. You may have opportunity to see a side of the parent the caseworker never sees. I don't think you should assume regularly the role of interpreter to the caseworker. The parent has to learn how to communicate with her. But perhaps you can help them get started talking on a subject.

Never conceal from the caseworker anything you accidentally learn about the parent that will affect the child's welfare, and never agree to keep such a confidence from her. If you have ethical problems with this, remember that you are taking care of the child and your first responsibility is to the child. If the mother says, "I'll tell you something if you promise to keep it a secret," you should say, "No, I can't promise that, but I will promise to do what I think is right and what I think is best for Joey."

**Don't overreact to criticism.** Another thing that sometimes disturbs foster parents is a tendency on the part of parents to belittle or undercut them. The foster parent must develop enough toughness and understanding to take this in stride. The specific complaint is usually petty—maybe the parent finds something to criticize about the way the child is dressed when she visits. Or in your presence the parent encourages the child to complain about his situation, and promises all this will change when he returns home.

Try to remember that the parent knows that you are doing the job she should be doing, and that merely your existence is difficult for her to accept. The less adequately she was doing the job—and the more her personal inadequacy rather than circumstances is the cause of the child's being in foster care—the more picky she may be with you. Just don't let it get under your skin—and don't take it out on the child. If it is a persistent problem, you should say quite matter-of-factly that you are doing the best you can and that her criticisms make it harder for you to help her child. I doubt if this will do much good, but it might make you feel better. I surely wouldn't rebuke the mother in the child's hearing. The child may be feeling uncomfortable about the parent's complaints, and torn between two loyalties.

I do not want to imply that getting to know these parents is all problems and all giving on your part. It can be an experience that tremendously enriches your life. Many parents are coping with problems beyond the magnitude of anything we have experienced. There are varying degrees of success, but I have found much to wonder at and admire. I can guarantee that you will come to feel quite uncomfortable listening to average after-dinner discussions about "the people on welfare."

# 8

# Parental Visits

Visitation rules are usually at the discretion of the caseworker. She may be guided by directions set down by the court for a particular child, or by agency policies. In addition, she must consider the welfare of the parents and the child. She would like to have the visits such that they do not interfere greatly with the child's adjustment to you and your home. No wonder that in this maze of persons to be satisfied or taken into account, problems sometimes arise in connection with parental visits.

To avoid confusion it is well to consider the purposes of the parental visits. To some extent they are always the same, but on a particular visit one goal may overshadow others. Following are some possibilities.

The child will be returning home soon, and parental visits have been stepped up to enable the parent and child to get better used to each other before the move is made.

The parent is ill and physically unable to care for the child, but loves the child and wants to remain in close touch.

An effort is being made to rebuild the family, and visits with the child motivate the parents to keep trying so that he can return home.

There are all sorts of variations and possibilities. When any of the clear-cut reasons mentioned exist, it is fairly easy for the foster family to accept the visits and cooperate with them.

Here are some possibilities that are likely to make it difficult for you to accept parental visits.

The parent does not want full responsibility for the child but also does not want to feel she has abandoned him. Through visits she maintains this ambiguous role.

The parent is immature and has not really accepted her role as parent. She comes to visit the child almost as though the child were a toy to be played with.

The parent feels social pressure to visit her child, or the child is putting pressure on her.

The second set of reasons seems on the surface so inadequate that it would seem easy to say visits should not be permitted, especially if they cause emotional upsets in the foster family. But in a long-term view, these visits may be even more important than those for the reasons first listed. Remember that in ordinary instances, the goal is the return of the child to his family. If this is going to happen, some semblance of family structure must be maintained. Family relationships must be strengthened, not weakened. Being a foster parent involves learning to handle constructively your part in this endeavor.

The mechanics of parental visits are worked out by the caseworker after talking with you, and considering what is possible for the parent.

If the parent has unlimited visiting privileges, the frequency of visits depends mainly on what happens to the child as a result of the visits. Of course, the foster parent has a right to limit how much time an extra person is around, just for your own sake. In our experience, parents have tended to visit less often than we felt necessary for the child, but that may not be the case with you. Of course, if every visit resulted in 3 days of upsetting reactions in the child and the parents came once or twice a week, visits would have to be cut back until they could be handled better by the child.

It will have to be decided whether visits are to be made in your home, or in the parents' home. Some policy will have to be discussed regarding special outings.

**How to make home visits work.** If the visits are made in your home, there are some practices that will help to make those visits successful from the viewpoint of both parents and child.

Unless the caseworker has asked you to sit in on visits, you should arrange to give the parents and child some privacy. You can go on about your work, do a yard job, or make a fairly private room available. You can't be rigid about this and you will have to be sensitive to the situation.

If the parent-child relationship is strained, it may help if you and the child consider in advance something he and his parents can do together. For some people it is awkward just to sit and talk; some minor activity may help them relax. Once conversation starts, the activity may be forgotten. In the case of young children, I try to put out toys that the child enjoys and that the parent can use in playing with the child.

If you are going to develop a partnership relation with the parents in caring for the child, it helps to give the parent some time to talk with you. You may want to prepare the child in advance, being careful about what you say. Tell him your purpose is to get to know him better by what his parents can tell you about him, and to get to know his parents better. Then stick to those purposes. I don't think you should report to the parents on the child, though I would encourage the child to tell the parents about his affairs himself. Of course you will answer honestly general questions about his health and progress.

Remember that especially during the first few visits, a mother may feel awkward in your home. You are strangers, and she is there because she must come if she wishes to see her child. Try to make her feel welcome, on her own account, because she is the child's mother and because you want to know her. (Fathers visit too, though perhaps infrequently; father visits do not often take place in your home.) The mother may assume that you know all about her personal life, and since she probably knows nothing about yours, may feel at a disadvantage. Your home may be nicer than what she is used to, and the strangeness may make her uncomfortable. Do as you would for any guest—offer her a cup of coffee or some other symbol of hospitality, be natural and not overly intimate. She usually will relax and the visit will become less of a strain for both of you.

*Tape D*

**Advantages of home visits.** The practice of encouraging the parents to visit the child in his foster home has some distinct advantages. They are worth considering when you make plans with the caseworker.

In general, visits in his everyday surroundings seem to be less over-stimulating to the child. The younger the child, the more this seems to be true. Just having to get dressed for a ride, go some place, return and settle in again, is more exhausting than if his parents come to see him. If the child has a cold or the weather is bad, it will not be necessary to cancel or rearrange the visit on the child's account.

Visiting the child where he lives gives much more opportunity for the child to share his present life with his parents. He can show his mother his latest school papers, plan to introduce her to a friend in the neighborhood, or make plans to have her meet his teacher. This helps to make the period in foster care less of an isolated interval and more a part of his life before and after foster care.

Home visits give the mother an opportunity to observe how you relate to her child. Assuming that you have had the opportunity to learn and have profited by experience, you may be able to help the mother in child-rearing skills. You don't necessarily have to say a word directly to the mother. For example, you might have to correct the child for interrupting you as you talk with the mother. That you do so, that you do so firmly, yet courteously, and that the child accepts your correction (I hope he does this time!) will make an impression. Or perhaps, when the child asks for a cookie, you repeat your rule about not eating a half hour before dinner, and you stick to it with good-natured firmness, even if the child whines. We had a little girl once who cried a great deal and whose parents had got in the habit of punishing her excessively for misdeeds. It became apparent to them on the very first visit that they had been expecting far too much of a toddler. The mother was quick to observe what we permitted, and was pleased to see her child happier. She modified her parenting accordingly, to the benefit of the child.

Home visits give you an opportunity to observe how the parent relates to the child. This may solve some puzzling questions for you and give you the background you need to understand the child's behavior.

If I seem to have made foster parents sound superior, remember that this is not a case of foster parents doing everything right and natural parents doing everything wrong. But your home has been chosen for foster care because it was believed to be a good place for a child, and the child may have had to leave his own home because it was not a good place for him. The purpose is not to prove superiority—it is to help. You cannot help by glossing over or ignoring the difficulties his parents' behavior has caused the child.

**Problems in home visits.** Having listed the advantages of home visits, we should also consider some of the problems that arise fairly regularly.

Sometimes parents and foster parents get into a quandary as to who should be in charge of the child during the visit. Since most children will test a new situation to see what they can get away with, you may wind up with considerable misbehavior. You may be uncertain as to how your correcting the child will look to the mother, or whether your action may make her feel like an outsider when you want her to feel comfortable. You hesitate to act as promptly as you otherwise would.

At the same time the parent may feel somewhat ashamed of the behavior, but reluctant to do anything in your home. Or she may over-react and, because it is your home, punish the child for something the child knows the mother usually lets him get away with. Children are experts at putting adults on the hook. With a matter-of-fact explanation to the parent if it is the first visit or the second, I try to act exactly as I would if the parent were not there. The child catches on in a hurry and the air is cleared. The approach should be that you are the parents in the house, that the child is expected to live by your standards of behavior while with you, and that you will see that he does. Trying to switch back and forth according to the adults around just confuses a child.

Occasionally a parent appears for a scheduled home visit with a plan to take the child somewhere. (You should ask when the child is placed what you are to do in such a situation.) I suggest that you reject the plan, unless you had previous permission from the caseworker to grant such a request. If you have been given the authority to make the decision, you will have to do so according to your best judgment on short notice. If the replacing of home visits with trips outside the home becomes habitual, you should discuss it with the caseworker. If you forbid a trip and the parent is displeased, you may be able to get her to talk to the caseworker about visiting arrangements. Perhaps it is time for a change.

Another problem arises when visits are not made on schedule. It is an inconvenience to have a parent appear at the door on a day you had a multitude of other things to get done. If it is difficult for the parent to make and keep plans (irregular workings hours or transportation difficulties) ask her to telephone you about visits as far ahead as she can. Try to get her to set a schedule. It will make life easier for everyone and may be good training for a disorganized parent.

Parent failure to make scheduled visits can be so devastating to a child that something must be done about it. The parent must be told by you or the caseworker what a skipped visit means to the child. Sometimes foster children make up absurd stories to explain why they do not live with their parents. They must constantly shore up the belief that their parents love them. Imagine how a child feels if, after he has told his schoolmates that his mother is coming to see him, a buddy comes home with him to meet the mother, and she fails to show up. Please try to do something right away about a situation where scheduled visits are skipped. Of course, the child has to learn to accept an occasional disappointment and with your help he will learn to do so.

Extra visits can also be wearing on your family and interfere with the child's adjustment to your home. You should ask the caseworker for help in stopping such visits.

Under some circumstances, you and the caseworker may agree that some or all of the parental visits should be made elsewhere than in the foster home. The caseworker may arrange to pick the child up and take him to the parents' home, the parents may do so, or trips may be taken in the company of the parents, with or without the caseworker. Occasionally visits are arranged in a neutral place such as a church visiting room, or at the agency itself.

**Advantages of out-of-the-home visits.** Regardless of how hard everybody tries to make home visits work, it is sometimes difficult for all to relax. The older child senses the ambiguity of the situation, even if he cannot express this in words, and may dread visits because of the emotional discomfort they cause him. Getting you and your home out of the picture may help to make the visit better serve its purpose of maintaining and strengthening the relationships between the parents and their child.

When representatives of both sets of parents are on hand, the child may feel he is in a double bind. If the parental sets are different in what they want him to be, he may feel pulled two ways as he tries to please both. Or he may decide it is hopeless and give up trying to please either. You as foster parents are working toward establishing a set of values he has accepted as his own, to guide him. While these values are developing it may help not to put him in situations where he feels under stress.

Out-of-home visits also give the child a chance to keep in touch with the home to which he expects to return. The physical surroundings remain familiar, the people in the neighborhood still know him.

These visits also give the parents an opportunity to provide some extras for the child, and this may help them to feel less hopeless about themselves as parents. The child also can let the parents know what he needs and likes and they can learn to enjoy doing things together.

**Problems of out-of-home visits.** Problems seem to originate in out-of-home visiting just as often as in home visits.

As mentioned earlier, just the process of going somewhere is more stimulating to children than a home visit. In addition, the activities may wear the child out and leave him emotionally or physically exhausted. This happens especially when the visit turns into an excursion into the delights of childhood. If the caseworker is providing transportation, you can expect her to place some restraints. But it is fairly common to get the child back to your home overtired and stuffed with chocolate bars and peanut brittle. I don't blame you for being provoked if you are then up all night with a sick youngster. Be sure the corrective action you take supports the parent's good intentions.

Out-of-home visits also may take place in what is basically an artificial physical setting. Neither parent nor child will do much communicating if the time together is spent seeing a movie. The setting can also be artificial emotionally. Both parent and child may see the visit only as an interruption of their real lives, and just kill the time together instead of using it to strengthen their ties. Given an excess of outside activity, parents and child may successfully avoid meaningful intimacy. Nothing in the physical setting may serve as a connection to everyday life.

If the opportunity to visit the child is turned frequently into a pleasure trip or a shopping excursion, another problem may surface. The situation tends to place the foster parents in the role of providers of mundane necessities and overseers of daily drudgery. By contrast, treats, delights, and hours of freedom come from his own parent. Since life normally mixes these two elements, this is an unrealistic and harmful division. You may need the help of the caseworker in getting the parent to understand the problem and help to solve it. In exercising discipline and accepting daily responsibility for the child, you cannot surrender the right to reward the child with special treats. If he can turn to his own parents for them without regard to his behavior with you, your approval will not be so important to him as it should be. This situation tends to make the child a manipulator of people, including his parents, for what he can get from them materially.

Out-of-home visits that involve material advantage to the foster child over the foster siblings can cause jealousy between them. It is obvious to your children that you are trying to give the foster child a life equal to their own—to make him part of the family. Frequent bonuses for only the foster child will not promote harmony. Since the parent needs the satisfaction of providing for the child, it is best if the gifts are needed things. The child's joy in them can come from the fact that his parent chose and paid for them. I would make special excursions few and far between, and take trips when all of your children can participate on the same basis.

Some problems arise or are aggravated because of your unacknowledged wish that the parents would not visit at all. The visits may be a reminder that you will have to give up the child some day. They require you to spend a couple of hours playing second fiddle in a concrete set of circumstances. Or the visits are difficult in themselves and upset the child's routine, while you want to keep things on an even keel.

Visiting by parents can never be completely satisfactory to you or to them, because the whole foster care arrangement is not completely satisfactory. But if it is the best solution to the problem of the child's care that can be found at present, an effort should be made to minimize the problems and make the visits as profitable as possible.

*GROWING*
*THROUGH FOSTER PARENTING*

# 9

# Personal and Family Growth

The year we reentered the foster care program our youngest daughter had completed first grade. I had tried a brief office stint, returning to the insurance work of early married years. A job outside the home just did not work for me and I did not find the job stimulating enough to effect the adjustments that would make it work. I tried filling the extra hours with volunteer work, but much of what I did was "busy" work, and I have an aversion to committee meetings. I thought of going back to school but I had no particular goal in mind, and if I were to study only things that interested me, I could do that on my own without the regimen of term papers and pop quizzes. Foster care seemed an opportunity to use my time in worthwhile ways, and my responsibilities in the home could be tied into these new responsibilities in a way that it would benefit the family. Except for brief periods of depression when a child leaves, foster care has been an enjoyable experience.

Reasons for entering foster care are uniquely yours. They vary with every individual and with every family. Perhaps your own children are reaching toward maturity and you feel that you have learned a great deal through rearing them. You would like to use your knowledge and experience for the benefit of other children. Perhaps you are searching for some way to make a worthwhile contribution of extra time and someone has told you about the need for intelligent and loving foster care.

Probably your personal reasons fit into this generalization: You entered foster care to benefit yourself, your family and the child.

If foster care is to contribute the maximum to your life, if foster care is to enrich and enlarge your family life, if foster care is to meet the needs of the child, you must consider what steps you will take to keep from stagnating in the routine care of children. This chapter deals with means you can use to make the experience rich and varied and a way to grow. Many of the following suggestions are particularly apt for foster mothers, others for both foster parents.

**Reevaluate your job.** In the first chapter of this book, emphasis was given to the problem of matching your abilities and resources to the kind of care you are giving and the age of the child you parent. As time passes your family may outgrow the arrangement you have made. It is important to reevaluate your situation from time to time, especially if the arrangement you have is beginning to get you down. Our family's arrangement keeps evolving—it is hard to say what we will be doing in a couple of years—and it is exciting to think about the possibilities.

**Stay fit.** Child care is hard work. Sometimes I read articles about the easy life I have compared with that of my grandmother. I am thankful for every modern appliance I have but I don't have one that changes diapers or carries children up and down stairs. Staying alert all day to the needs of little children takes concentration. In the evening, husband and teenagers appreciate a little enthusiasm for the time spent with them. As often as I can manage, I nap when the little ones do, and every night Don and I jog for 15 or 20 minutes around our neighborhood. No matter how tired I am I feel better after it. Rest, proper eating, and exercise are essential to the good health on which your capacity for mental life and growth usually is based.

**Share the load.** The bulk of day-to-day nurture of children will probably fall to the mother, but the father should not be excluded. Working together offers many opportunities to improve your understanding of each other as you try to help the child. You also may be pleasantly surprised to find a problem you couldn't solve yielding to your husband's efforts.

David was 3 years, 6 months old. The background of the problem was unknown to us, but when he reached our home he was adamantly opposed to going to sleep. He didn't just protest bedtime; he staged open rebellion and the process could mean an hour of kicking and screaming. None of my "tried and true" methods seemed to make a dent—in fact, he didn't respond to anything after a sentence including "bed." So Don assumed the task of putting him to bed. He used some of the same methods, said the same things, but apparently for David, being Dad and not Mother made a big difference. The improvement in the situation was satisfying to both of us, and provided a useful clue we could pass on to his new family.

**Involve your children.** Foster care will stimulate growth in the lives of your children if they are involved. I do not refer to physical care alone. Our girls have learned to change diapers and give baths like experts. But more important, they are in the process of learning what little children are like. They see firsthand the damage a harsh, unloving home can do, and they have the joy of seeing spirits mend as a result of care they help to give. The lessons are practical. A 2-year-old was kicking and screaming at me as I took her from the table. "Don't you just feel like slapping her?" "Yes, I do. But it wouldn't do anything but make her angrier and she is in no condition to learn anything from what I say now." Or "How could two married people start treating each other and their little kids like that?" The explanation is never simple, but an important part may be that the couple married just out of high school, before either had the maturity needed. We hope our children will profit for themselves, and also learn compassion and understanding for people in trouble.

**Read.** The experience of rearing children is almost universal, and the list of books on the subject is nearly endless. I have found it handy to have some available for reference; others are in public libraries and can be borrowed for one-time reading. Reading and discussing the books with others will help you understand yourself, as well as the children you care for. You can glean new ideas to try in specific situations, or find encouragement; parents like yourselves have faced apparently impossible situations, lived through the experience, and shared it in a book. As experienced parents, it is tempting to think we know the answers to our problems. But when a school principal was once complimented on the fact that he had working for him two teachers with 20 years of experience, he replied that he had one teacher with 20 years of experience and one teacher with 1 year of teaching experience 20 times repeated. Reading helps to keep minds alert and willing to try new ideas.

**Have some other interests.** No matter how interesting a job, it helps to have some other interests to occupy the mind some of the time. This is true of caring for children, too.

You ought to have some time off, just for yourself. If other members of the family cannot keep the children for you, a regular baby-sitter is a necessity. In our case, Grandma is next door and she makes it a point to give me free time. The children are used to her, she knows our routines and the arrangement works beautifully. Perhaps there is an older woman in your neighborhood who would like to be a foster grandma.

During the winter I sew, and during the growing season I garden. Both these hobbies are relaxing and fun, and can be pursued along with the care of children. Most children will get a kick out of a garment you make for them. A short row of carrots to watch grow, pull up, and eat is a wonderful thing to a child.

It helps me to spend part of my time with children of another age, and for a number of years leading a Junior Girl Scout troop has added a great deal to my life. Camping with the girls is a good change of pace; for regular meetings, they come to our basement. The foster children become honorary members of the troop.

My hobbies and interests surely won't fit your needs, but try to find some that will. They should fit into your life well enough that they don't seem "more trouble than they are worth."

**Get to know other foster parents.** Whether or not there is a formal group in your area, get acquainted with other parents involved in foster care. You can learn from each other, encourage each other—and get acquainted with some people you would not have met through job, church or neighborhood. The foster children you care for also learn that they are not unique, and since being different is hard on children at certain ages, this can mean a lot. Such contacts help them understand their own situation.

# 10

## Foster Parents and the Foster Care Program

The first responsibility you have as a foster parent is to be parent to the foster child. The amount of time you have to get involved formally in the broader aspects of the foster care program will vary, but you should have an idea of what needs to be done.

**Public relations.** I am using this term to describe all the activity that must be carried on to create a better public climate for foster care. You can become a source of accurate information about foster care. This includes answers to relatively unimportant questions such as "How many children are involved in the program in this county?" Or more important questions such as "Why don't these children get adopted instead of being left in foster care for years?" If I don't know the answer to a question and it concerns the program, (not a specific child, of course), I try to get it. Changes in the program are needed, and we require a base of informed public opinion.

Here is a concrete example of needed opinion change affecting some foster children. Of all the dentists in our community, only three accept Medicaid patients. Consequently, it becomes a major project to get dental care for children under this program. Local dentists must be made aware of the need we have for their cooperation.

**Join the Foster Parents Association.** Your participation in a foster parent association can further your own growth. The associations exist for three main reasons: to provide foster parents with a structure for the exchange of information and ideas; to encourage and help foster parents; and to work for changes in the foster care program that will benefit children and their families.

To achieve the first goal, regular meetings are held, libraries are maintained, study groups are organized, and community resources are analyzed and listed.

Encouragement and help are given on a person-to-person basis, either at meetings or through contacts made in the association.

The last aim covers a broad range of activities. It may involve taking steps to establish a grievance procedure in the local care program. It may involve working with local school officials to effect changes in enrollment policies. The hope is that united effort will achieve needed changes that parents acting individually cannot hope to bring about.

**Study the law governing the care of children.** Laws governing children in various types of care programs are varied and often vague. Test cases around the country are raising challenges to accepted practice. A trend is developing toward greater consideration of the "rights of the child" in custody conflicts. Many states have passed laws creating subsidized adoption where this would result in a happier situation for the child than a foster care arrangement. Though differing among states, the arrangements involve some kind of continuing money payments to enable certain children to be adopted by families of moderate means.

The courts will make some changes, legislators will make others, but the stimulus of informed foster parents is greatly needed. Foster parents know better than any others the disadvantages to foster children inherent in the program. Who more than we should seek the changes to minimize these disadvantages?

# APPENDIX

## *Foster Parents' Responsibilities and Obligations

1. To provide shelter, food, personal care including laundry, cleaning, toilet articles, haircuts, recreation, and to maintain clothing in clean and good condition. (Call the caseworker for clothing purchase order, and present it to the sales clerk. If you are given the sales slip, return it to the department with the child's name on it.)
2. To guide, discipline and give appropriate religious and/or moral training and to encourage participation in community activities.
3. To give tender loving care . . . the same type of care given to one's own children.
4. To provide for school attendance, educational needs, except school lunches, book rental and incidental supplies; to call any special educational needs to the attention of the caseworker; to encourage the development of any special talent the child may have.
5. To discuss with the caseworker emotional and/or behavioral factors that may affect the planning for the child.
6. To instruct and give example in good health and hygiene habits.
7. To provide an individual allowance for the child's spending money, based on the age of the child and the foster parent's decision.
8. To take care of the child as long as he is in need of foster care. (If

---

* From the handbook for parents prepared by the Foster Parents Association of Tippecanoe County, Lafayette, Indiana.

circumstances in the foster home are altered through accidents or illness such that it is impractical or impossible to care for the child, other arrangements can be made.)

9. To accompany a child in need of medical and/or dental services to the family physician or dentist. (The doctor or dentist should be informed that the agency will pay for the services rendered. The agency will be billed by the doctor, dentist and pharmacist for the services. Prior authorization is needed from the welfare department for the services of an eye doctor. Where a legal guardian is required to sign, authorization from the department must be obtained for all medical and dental care. Such authorization is not needed for routine office calls except for eye care.)

10. To keep a medical record of the child.

11. To notify the agency of a change of address or telephone number.

12. To report any change in the family living arrangements.

13. To discuss plans with the caseworker before boarding or lodging other children or adults in the home.

14. To permit visitation by the child's own parents when this is arranged by the County Department of Public Welfare after consultation with the foster parents.

15. To notify the agency before taking the child for extended trips in time or distance; to consult with the caseworker about any extended baby-sitting arrangements.

16. To assume financial responsibility if a child under 18 obtains a driver's license. (The Welfare Department cannot assume financial responsibility. The foster parent must check with the Welfare Department before consenting to a driver's permit or license.)

## °Agency's Responsibilities and Obligations

1. To act as the legal guardian for foster care.

2. To provide all necessary expenses for medical and dental care and for eye examinations and glasses.

3. To provide for psychological and/or educational testing when this seems appropriate.

4. To provide clothing according to the age and sex of the child.

5. To provide school lunches, book rental and incidental school supplies, and special education help as needed.

---

° From the handbook for parents prepared by the Foster Parents Association of Tippecanoe County, Lafayette, Indiana.

6. To make arrangements for visits with the child's own parents or relatives when appropriate.
7. To provide the foster home with guidance, cooperating in the best interest of the child.
8. To provide each foster parent with an identification card containing emergency names and telephone numbers.
9. To consult with foster parents regarding authorization for foster children to take driver's training or obtain a driver's license.
10. To provide the foster parents with information about the child's background that will be helpful in guiding the child, i.e., previous behavior problems, attitudes, reasons why the child left previous home or homes, etc.
11. To provide the foster parents with a letter of awareness when the family is on an extended leave from the community.